Presented To:

_____

_____

From:

_____

_____

Date:

_____

...And Then He Called My Name

The Tragedy and Triumph of the Cross Like You've Never Experienced It Before

Richard Exley

WHITE STONE BOOKS

LAKELAND, FLORIDA

07 06 05 04 03   10 9 8 7 6 5 4 3 2 1

...And Then He Called My Name
The Tragedy and Triumph of the Cross Like
You've Never Heard It Before
ISBN 1-59379-017-1
Copyright © 2004, 1996 by Richard Exley
P. O. Box 54744
Tulsa, Oklahoma 74155

Published by WhiteStone Books
P. O. Box 2835
Lakeland, Florida 33806

To Jesus Christ.
May Your kingdom come,
may Your will be done,
on earth as it is in heaven.

Contents

To the Reader

...*And Then He Called My Name* tells the "greatest story ever told" through the eyes of those who participated in it. Within the factual framework of Scripture, history, and tradition, I give my imagination free rein to create first-person, eyewitness accounts of both the crucifixion and the resurrection.

The power of these stories is in their ability to make you, the reader, a part of them. Instead of just reading about the passion of Jesus, you can experience it through the accounts of those who were there.

As a knowledgeable reader, you will readily recognize where Scripture ends and imagination begins. Yet because I have made my creativity congruent with the facts, I believe you will also recognize the reality of these accounts. The truth of these vignettes is not in the incidental "facts" which I have created, but in the reality of their universal humanity. This is how people feel in these kinds of circumstances. And this is why people do these kinds of things.

I have endeavored to make these accounts true to what we are as human beings. If I have succeeded, they will speak to you in a deeply personal, perhaps even life-changing way.

The Son

FOR THIS DAY

———

I WAS BORN, AND

———

FOR FOR THIS DAY CAME

———

I INTO THE WORLD.

CHAPTER ONE

For this reason was I born, and for this day came I into the world. Yet as the time draws near I find that I am overwhelmed. My soul literally recoils at what is before me. It is not the Roman cross I fear, nor the shame of being crucified with criminals, but separation from my heavenly Father.

Never have I displeased Him. Never have I felt the brunt of His holy anger. Soon all of that will change. Soon I will become the very thing He most detests.[1] Soon there will be a gulf between us and I will be the sole object of His unmitigated wrath.[2]

These thoughts weigh heavily upon me as I enter Gethsemane with the eleven disciples. It is a favorite retreat of mine, a place where I often come to be alone with the Father. Tonight it affords me no comfort. It is dark and foreboding, not at all like a place of prayer.

Turning to Peter, James, and John, I confide, "My soul is overwhelmed with sorrow to the point of death. Stay here and keep watch."[3]

Leaving them, I go a little farther before falling face down on the cold ground. I try to pray, but the words will not come. The will of the Father is clear, yet everything within me fights against it. I should pray for strength, for courage, but instead I plead with the Father. Desperately, I search for an alternative, for another way, a less extreme way, to fulfill His purpose.

> ...MORE THAN ANYTHING, I WANT TO PLEASE HIM.

Now I plead, "*Abba*, Father,...everything is possible for You. Take this cup from me. Yet not what I will, but what You will."[4]

Everything within me is repulsed by the cup which the Father presses upon me. Yet, more than anything, I want to please Him.

With trembling hands I lift it, look deep into its dark dregs. I am determined to drink it, but I cannot. What I see causes my soul to recoil in horror, and I stumble from the place of prayer, seeking the comfort of my friends.

To my amazement I find them sleeping. Grabbing Peter by the shoulder I shake him. "Could you not keep watch for one hour?"[5]

For once Peter is speechless. He doesn't know what to say,[6] and I cannot help but feel kindly toward him. Had he blustered or tried to make excuses, I might have rebuked him, but his grieving silence touches something deep in my heart. More gently I say, "Watch and pray so that you will not fall into temptation. The spirit is willing, but the body is weak."[7]

Returning to the place of prayer, a great heaviness settles upon me. The future is foreboding. Soon Judas will come and I will be placed under arrest. My disciples will desert me, fleeing in fear, and Peter will deny me. Caiaphas the High Priest and the Sanhedrin will charge me with blasphemy, a crime punishable by death. My own countrymen will scream for my blood. Pilate will order me scourged, and I will be beaten within an inch of my life. Finally, the Romans will nail me to a cross, and there I will die.

All of this is painful beyond imagining, yet it is not what my soul cannot bear. It is not what I plead for the Father to take from me. All of this I can manage because the Father will be with me. He will strengthen me. With the Father's help I can bear the injustice and brutality of men. What I cannot imagine, what my soul cringes at, is the prospect of being separated from Him and suffering the penalty for sin at His hand. Once more the Father presses the cup upon me, and try as I may I cannot bring myself to drink it. In its dark dregs is the poison that is destroying those who were created in His image. There is rebellion there, and lust, and profane passions. It is filled to the brim with all manner of evil — treachery and deceit, pride and power, adultery and murder. Sickness and disease are

> EVERYTHING THAT I HATE IS IN THAT CUP, EVERYTHING THAT I HAVE COME TO DESTROY.

there, as is death. Everything that I hate is in that cup, everything that I have come to destroy.

The Father's purpose is clear, but I cannot bring myself to accept His plan, at least not yet. Surely there must be another way.

"Father," I pray, while my inner turmoil causes my sweat to become like blood,[8] "if it is not possible for this cup to be taken away unless I drink it, may your will be done."[9]

Having said that, I flee the place of prayer to seek the support of my friends. Once more they are sleeping, and though my heart is grieved I do not wake them. Their companionship might provide a temporary solace, but in the end the cup is mine and mine alone. No one can share it with me.

For the third time I go to the Father. My anguish is almost unbearable, and I pray earnestly with tears and loud cries.[10] There is no other way, of that I am now sure. I must drink the cup of iniquity. I must become the thing I most hate in order to destroy it. I, who have been tempted in all ways without sin,[11] must now become sin in order to accomplish the Father's purpose.

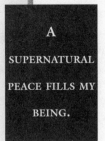

A SUPERNATURAL PEACE FILLS MY BEING.

With trembling hands I take the cup from the Father and place it to my lips. "May Your will be done," I pray, and drink deeply from its deadly dregs.

A supernatural peace fills my being. No longer am I at war with myself and the Father. Once more I am focused. My only reason for living is to accomplish His purpose. Like a flint, I set my face toward Golgotha.

Returning to the disciples for the third time I arouse them. My hour has come and through the trees I see the flickering light of several lanterns. Turning to the sleep-drugged disciples I say, "Here comes my betrayer!"[12]

Hardly are the words out of my mouth before Judas enters the clearing leading a group of armed temple guards.

Without hesitation he comes to me and greets me with a kiss. Before he can step away I grip him by the shoulders and look deep into his eyes.

"Judas," I ask in a voice they all can hear, "are you betraying the Son of Man with a kiss?"[13]

Jerking free of my grip he steps aside and I am instantly surrounded by the guards. Drawing his sword Peter strikes the man nearest him, cutting off his right ear.[14] Having expected no resistance, the guards fall back, momentarily confused.

Ordering Peter to put his sword away, I step toward the wounded man who is holding the side of his head and moaning. Even in the dark I can see that he is covered with blood. Stretching out my hand I gently touch his wound, instantly healing him.[15]

Having regrouped, the guards now spread out, cutting off all avenues of escape. Cautiously they move in, being careful to keep an eye on the eleven who have withdrawn a little to one side.

Holding my ground I challenge them. "Am I leading a rebellion, that you have come with swords and clubs? Every day I was with you in the temple courts, and you did not lay a hand on me. But this is your hour — when darkness reigns."[16]

In an instant they are upon me. Jerking my arms behind my back they bind my wrists securely.[17] I search for Judas, finally locating him in the deep shadows at the far edge of the clearing. Staring at him, I will him to look at me, but he will not. Already he has separated himself from me.

> THE NEXT TWELVE HOURS ARE HORRIBLE BEYOND ANYTHING I COULD HAVE IMAGINED.

The next twelve hours are horrible beyond anything I could have imagined. I suffer every way it is possible for a human being to suffer — physically, mentally, and emotionally. Nevertheless, through it all I am sustained by the Father's presence and the supernatural peace which He gives. Even on the cross I find the strength to intercede for my executioners.

Suddenly at the sixth hour darkness falls.[18] Though it is high noon, it is blacker than a moonless night. The sun cannot penetrate the darkness, nor the stars, and it is impossible to see. Black as it is, this physical darkness cannot compare to the dark night which descends upon my soul.

In the darkness the Father deals with me, not as a loving and merciful father with his child, but as the Righteous Judge with an evildoer. He now regards me as the greatest sinner to be found beneath the sun and discharges on me the whole weight of His wrath.

In the void I hear Him say, "Depart from Me," and I experience a punishment worse than death — separation from God. As inconceivable as it seems, in surrendering to the will of the Father I have accepted the one thing I cannot bear — His rejection! It is the price I must pay in order to redeem Adam's lost race, but it is nearly more than I can endure. Never in time or eternity have I been separated from Him. Never, until this moment.

Somewhere in the deepest recesses of my tormented soul an orphan's cry is born. *"Eloi, Eloi, lama sabachthani?...My God, my God, why have you forsaken me?"*[19]

There is no answer for God is gone, and I am alone. Totally alone.

Death is very near, and in the gloom the prince of darkness, the keeper of the dead, gloats as he waits for me to die. Summoning the last of my swiftly ebbing strength, I cry, "Father, into your hands I commit my spirit."[20]

> AT LAST IT IS FINISHED. THE CUP IS FINALLY EMPTY. SIN'S DEBT HAS BEEN PAID.

At last it is finished. The cup is finally empty. Sin's debt has been paid. I have suffered the full penalty for the sins of all mankind. Now the Father is free to pardon and forgive even the worst of Adam's lost race.

For further study, see Life Lessons from Chapter One.

The Betrayer

HE HAD A WAY OF

SPEAKING UNLIKE ANYONE

I HAD EVER HEARD.

CHAPTER TWO

Having delivered Jesus into the hands of the chief priests as per our agreement, I now watch as the temple guards bind his hands and prepare to lead him away. I should have a sense of triumph, or at least some feeling of accomplishment, but I don't. Instead I feel strangely empty. Not guilty, just unfulfilled.

Against my will my mind returns to an earlier time when hope was as bright as the summer sun. In those days I believed Jesus could do anything. He had a way of speaking unlike anyone I had ever heard. When he talked about the Father, or the kingdom, my heart fairly leaped within me. He made it all seem so immediate, so real. There were even moments when I could almost believe that he was the chosen One. At those times, like Peter, I wanted to shout, 'You are the Christ, the Son of the living God.'[1]

For all his gifts, Jesus was incredibly naive. A politically astute person would have built on his popularity and seized the moment. But not Jesus! There were several times, especially during the early months of his ministry, when the masses were determined to make him a king. What did he do? He went into hiding, disappearing for weeks at a time. We tried to reason with him, but to no avail.

Although he talked about his kingdom constantly, even promising we would "sit on twelve thrones judging the twelve tribes of Israel,"[2] every time he had a chance to become king he threw it away. After awhile it seemed there was no connection between what he said and what he did, at least with regard to his kingdom.

With an effort I dismiss all thoughts of what might have been. It is too late for that and I will not torment myself with idle speculation now. I have made my decision, cast my lot with the elders and chief priests. Let others judge me if they will, I know I did the only sensible

> LET OTHERS JUDGE ME IF THEY WILL, I KNOW I DID THE ONLY SENSIBLE THING UNDER THE CIRCUMSTANCES, DIFFICULT THOUGH IT WAS.

thing under the circumstances, difficult though it was.

A surly guard now prods Jesus with the butt of his spear and we move out. Leaving Gethsemane we enter Jerusalem and make our way toward the home of Annas[3] the former high priest. Though he is now an old man, of more than seventy years, he is not without power. Through his influence five of his sons have occupied the office of high priest and Caiaphas, who is married to his daughter, currently holds that position. To the discerning, there is little doubt that he is the real authority behind the office.

As we wind our way through the dark streets, one of the temple guards positions himself at my shoulder. "What's he really like?" he asks, nodding his head in the direction of Jesus.

Being in no mood for small talk I ignore him, hoping he will go away. Unfortunately, he seems oblivious to my reticence, and after awhile he tries again. "I've heard rumors about miracles and such like," he says. "What do you know about that?"

"Little enough," I say. Though if the truth be known the miracles of Jesus are too numerous to be numbered.[4]

His disappointment is plain enough, but I am not about to get into this. The memories are still too fresh, and capable of invoking the very feelings from which I have tried so hard to distance myself. Talking about it can serve no good purpose.

Finally we arrive at the former high priest's house. Two of the temple guards escort Jesus inside where he is confronted by Annas and some of the elders. Our purpose in coming is not clear. Nothing official can be done here since Annas has no legal authority. Most likely the old man is simply curious about Jesus and desires to question him personally. Outside we huddle in small groups, talking in hushed voices. In short order Jesus is led back into the courtyard

> ALTHOUGH SECRET TRIALS ARE STRICTLY FORBIDDEN BY OUR LAW, IT NOW SEEMS OBVIOUS THAT THIS IS EXACTLY WHAT CAIAPHAS HAS IN MIND.

where he is immediately surrounded by a contingent of armed guards. This time there are no lanterns or torches, and an order is given to maintain absolute silence. According to the captain, it is imperative we attract no attention as we make our way toward the house of the high priest.

All of this secrecy can only mean one thing — they intend to try Jesus tonight. Although secret trials are strictly forbidden by our law, it now seems obvious that this is exactly what Caiaphas has in mind. It makes sense. Who knows what might happen if the multitudes were to awaken in the morning and find Jesus in the hands of the elders and the chief priests. But, if the trial is finished before daybreak and Jesus is already in the custody of the Romans, the Sanhedrin will have little or nothing to fear. Arriving at the house of the high priest, Jesus is immediately taken into a large semicircular room where the Sanhedrin is already in session. Though I remain outside, the proceedings in the lighted interior are clearly visible, being separated from the courtyard only by a row of pillars. Moving to the far wall, I squat in the shadows and draw my cloak about me against the cold. From here I can observe both the courtyard and the proceedings without being conspicuous. It soon becomes apparent that things are not going well for the elders. Although some hasty efforts have been made to assemble witnesses, they are hardly creditable.[5]

WITNESS AFTER WITNESS IS HEARD, YET THE SANHEDRIN CAN FIND NO EVIDENCE WITH WHICH TO CONDEMN JESUS.

A movement in the dark catches my eye, and I watch as John moves toward the outer door of the courtyard. Furtively he glances over his shoulder before opening the door. A large man emerges from the shadows beyond the wall and quickly steps inside. For an instant he is framed in the light. With a start I realize that it is Simon Peter.[6]

What is he doing here? Surely he can't be crazy enough to try to rescue Jesus. Such an attempt would be ludicrous. Still, I cannot help thinking it is just the kind of thing Peter might attempt. One thing is certain, I dare not show my face while he is around.

Moving deeper into the shadows I turn my attention back to the ecclesiastical trial. In dismay I watch as our carefully laid plans seem to unravel before my eyes. Witness after witness is heard, yet the Sanhedrin can find no evidence with which to condemn Jesus. Finally Caiaphas takes matters into his own hands.

Rising from his elevated seat he addresses Jesus in his most judicial manner. "I charge you under oath by the living God: Tell us if you are the Christ, the Son of God."[7]

Instantly the atmosphere in the room changes. The weariness and frustration of the long night give way to a sudden tension. Around the room the elders and chief priests lean forward. They sense Jesus himself may provide the condemning evidence they have not been able to produce. Caiaphas remains standing, towering over Jesus, willing him to incriminate himself.

Only Jesus seems unmoved by the drama of the moment. Yet he too is different, energized somehow. It is a transformation I have seen before. I saw it first when he commanded the storm to cease,[8] and again when he raised the widow's son from the dead.[9] Still, I have never sensed such transcendent authority, not even when he commanded Lazarus to come forth.[10]

...AND NOW THE MAGNITUDE OF WHAT I HAVE DONE HITS ME FOR THE FIRST TIME.

"Yes, it is as you say," Jesus replies, his voice clear and distinct. "But I say to all of you: In the future you will see the Son of Man sitting at the right hand of the Mighty One and coming on the clouds of heaven."[11]

In an instant the high priest gnashes his teeth and tears his robe, nearly beside himself with self-righteous rage. "He has spoken blasphemy!" he screams. "Why do we need any more witnesses?"[12]

With one voice the Sanhedrin answers, "He is worthy of death!"[13]

Suddenly the hatred and jealousy they have harbored these many months erupt. Rushing forward, they deposit huge wads of foul spittle full in his face. Others strike him with their fists, screaming, "Prophesy to us, Christ. Who hit you?"[14]

My reaction is different. It is not blasphemy I have heard, but prophetic revelation, and now the magnitude of what I have done hits me for the first time. It is not an impostor I have delivered into the hands of the religious authorities, but the Messiah. I have betrayed the chosen One of God! In stunned disbelief I watch from the shadows as the guards bind Jesus and prepare to deliver him to Pontius Pilate. Although his beard is stiff with spittle and his face bruised and bleeding, there is about him a sense of dignity that dwarfs his accusers.

"Wait!" I scream leaping to my feet and rushing toward the high priest.

For just a moment our eyes meet. In his there is a flicker of recognition, then he turns away in disgust. In that instant I see my condemnation written in his face. He has

TO MY EVERLASTING SHAME I DISCOVER THAT THE DEED AND I ARE ONE!

played me for a fool. Now that I am of no further use to him, I am of no more value than a leper in the streets, or a gentile.

"Wait!" I scream again, trying to force my way through the temple guards who block my way.

Reaching inside my garment I grab the bag of silver coins and thrust it toward the priests. "Take these," I plead. "Let Jesus go. He has done nothing worthy of death."

Ignoring the coins, they restrain me as Jesus is led away. When finally I am released I rush desperately from priest to priest begging, "Help me for I have sinned. I have betrayed innocent blood."[15] It is no use. They will not hear me. My desperate pleas fall on deaf ears.

Finally one of them says with a sneer, "What is that to us? That's your responsibility."[16]

His words are like a dagger plunged into my heart. Grabbing the silver coins, I hurl them at their feet before rushing into the street.[17]

Now the awful weight of my treachery descends upon me afresh and I stagger beneath the burden of my sin. It isn't just what I did — unspeakable though it was — but what I am. To my everlasting shame I discover that the deed and I are one!

I am driven to flee, to run away, but where can I go? The thing I cannot escape, the thing I cannot bear, is myself. So this is hell, I think, to live forever with what I have done.

Stumbling through the streets the words of Jesus return to haunt me. "The Son of Man will go just as it has been written about him. But woe to that man who betrays the

Son of Man![18] It would be better for him if he had not been born."[19]

I curse the day of my birth and the breasts that nursed me. I curse the day I heard the name of Jesus. I curse the high priest and the Roman governor. I curse my own life. In absolute despair I scream, "I am damned! I am damned!"

> THAT'S WHAT I CANNOT BEAR. NOT HIS ANGER, BUT HIS LOVE.

After a long time I find myself on the side of a steep hill overlooking a deep ravine. A rope is in my hand and on one end I have fashioned a hangman's noose. In a trancelike state, I loop the other end over a branch, being careful to place it as far out as I can reach. When it is securely tied I drop the noose over my head and draw it tight around my neck.

Closing my eyes I try to remember my mother's face but I cannot. Instead his eyes stare at me, not in anger, but with a wounded love. The way he looked at me when I kissed him in Gethsemane. That's what I cannot bear. Not his anger, but his love. Even now he seems to be calling to me. I am sobbing now. Weeping like a motherless child, but it is no use. Tears cannot save me. It is too late. Too late.

Regardless of what others may think, I know I did not consciously choose to become what I am. It was a subtle process and who can say what small act opened the door to the evil within? But once that door was open, it was impossible to close it again and now I must pay for what I have done.

With all my strength I scream, "I have sinned. I have betrayed the innocent blood of my Lord." Then I leap from the cliff[20] and in that final instant before death claims me it seems I hear him calling my name.

"Judas," he says. "Judas...."

For further study, see Life Lessons from Chapter Two.

The Governor

THESE LAST MONTHS

HAVE SEEN ONE CRISIS AFTER ANOTHER,

ALL POTENTIALLY DISASTROUS

TO MY CAREER.

CHAPTER THREE

Stepping out onto the balcony, I pretend to ignore the mob gathered in the street below, while studying the situation out of the corner of my eye. They're all here, from Caiaphas the high priest on down, so it must be important, though I cannot imagine what it is this time.

These last months have seen one crisis after another, all potentially disastrous to my career. The worst was probably the Jew's reaction when the Imperial Guard came into the city bearing Caesar's image upon their ensigns. "No images!" they screamed through the streets. "We will not condone the idolatrous image of Caesar in our midst."

For six days the angry crowds continued to grow, clamoring vehemently for the removal of Caesar's banners. It was a direct challenge to my authority, and one I dared not ignore. But in the end it proved disastrous.

The military forces I sent to disperse them only made them angrier, and they refused to be intimidated. Much to my astonishment they threw themselves upon the ground and bared their necks, willing to die rather than to see their religious laws transgressed.[1]

What could I do but back down? If I had slaughtered hundreds of Jews I would have never heard the end of it.

Some, political enemies for the most part, have suggested that such incidents were of my own making. "Pontius Pilate," they say, "is stubborn and insensitive. He creates his own problems."

> "PONTIUS PILATE," THEY SAY, "IS STUBBORN AND INSENSITIVE. HE CREATES HIS OWN PROBLEMS."

I hardly think so! How could I know the extremes to which these fanatical Jews would go?

Sighing deeply I run a hand over my face. I hate this place — the heat, the dust, the noise, and the squalor. Most of all I despise these mad Jews and their religious fanaticism. I find their blood sacrifices and intolerance utterly abhorrent. When I finish this term I will not accept another, no matter how persuasive the Emperor Tiberius is. Let him find someone else to govern this god-forsaken place.

Am I surprised that the Jews are back again? Hardly. It is a pattern with them, an obsession really. They can never leave well enough alone. Always they must attempt to bend me to their will.

Although Caiaphas and his self-righteous band of religious fanatics have come to the fortress Antonia, I still must accommodate their religious prejudice. It is Passover week, and they will not defile themselves by entering the "unclean" house of a Gentile. No matter that I am made to feel like the scum of the earth. Still, I must not offend their Jewish sensibilities lest they appeal to Herod, and he in turn appeal to Caesar. That must not happen again. Caesar himself has made that clear enough.

The cause of all this commotion seems to be a rather nondescript peasant. He is bound and closely guarded, though he does not appear at all dangerous. Not a revolutionist from the looks of him, besides the Jews would never turn in one of their own.

"What has this man done?" I demand, not even trying to keep the impatience out of my voice.

"He's a criminal," they respond patronizingly. "Why else would we bring him to you?"

Getting a straight answer out of these Jews is like trying to make a virgin out of a prostitute. But then two can play at this game.

Turning on my heel I head back inside. "Take care of him yourselves," I snap. "If he's one of you, judge him by your own law."

It's a dangerous game I play, but this time I win. Their bluff called, they hastily shout after me.

"He's plotting a rebellion against Rome and telling our people not to pay taxes to Caesar. He even claims to be king of the Jews."

> "HE EVEN CLAIMS TO BE KING OF THE JEWS."

Once back inside the palace I find that I am sweating, and not surprisingly either. With these Jews it is always a game of nerves. They have so little real power, yet they make so much of it. Grudgingly, I concede that they are a worthy foe.

Though I would like to ignore them, I know I cannot. If I take no action, and it turns out this peasant is really a revolutionist, Caesar will have my head. Still, I take a perverse pleasure in letting them wait.

At last I turn to a guard. "Bring the prisoner to me. I want to interrogate him privately."

Directly I hear the guard return with the prisoner, but I do not turn around or in any way acknowledge his presence. It is, I have found, an effective way to make a prisoner sweat.

When, at length, I confront him, he is not sweating. In fact, of everyone — Roman and Jew alike, myself included — he seems the only one at peace. He is no ordinary peasant, of that I am sure.

T H E G O V E R N O R

He has been beaten about the face and head, but not too badly. I wait for him to speak, to make his case. Instead, he simply looks at me, not defiantly, though it is obvious that he is not intimidated.

"Are you the king of the Jews?" I ask in a confidential tone, hoping to take him into my confidence.

"That depends on what you mean by king," he replies calmly.

Why am I not surprised? He is a Jew and they all talk in riddles.

"Let's not play word games," I respond, taking command. "I have no patience for it."

Looking at me intently he says, "My kingdom is not of this world."

"So you are a king then," I press him, hoping for a speedy resolution to this tiresome mess.

"For that reason I was born. And for that reason I came into the world. I speak truth, and everyone who loves truth receives me."

42

Raising one eyebrow I sneer, "What is truth?"[2]

This peasant is no king, at least not in any way that makes him a threat to Caesar. There's not a political bone in his body. He's innocent of their charges, but it will not be easy to release him. They are determined to see him put to death, though I can't imagine why.

Nearing the door to the balcony I am still weighing my options when I am hailed by my wife's personal servant. "Master," she calls, "an urgent message from your wife."

Taking her note I read it quickly. "Do not allow Caiaphas to draw you into his trap. In a dream I have seen that this man is innocent. If you judge him otherwise, you will suffer the consequences."[3]

Despite the stifling heat a chill runs up my spine and I cannot stop my hand from trembling.

Crumpling her disturbing note, I step onto the balcony and declare in a loud voice: "I have examined this man, and I do not find him guilty of any crime. Therefore I will have him scourged, and then I will release him."[4]

To my way of thinking this should satisfy their thirst for blood. The Roman whip is made of nine tails of leather, braided with bits of bone and iron. It is brutal, and only the strong survive it. Roman law normally forbids the scourging of an innocent person, but I believe it is a reasonable compromise. Better to be scourged than to be crucified.

"No!" the angry crowd screams. "This man is an enemy of Caesar."

Holding up my hands for silence I quiet the crowd. "It is customary," I remind them, "to release a prisoner each year at the time of the Passover. I will release this man to you." While we have been discussing the matter, the religious leaders have been working their way through the crowd. Now, as with one voice, the people began to chant: "Give us Barabbas! Give us Barabbas!"[5]

> ROMAN LAW NORMALLY FORBIDS THE SCOURGING OF AN INNOCENT PERSON, BUT I BELIEVE IT IS A REASONABLE COMPROMISE.

In disgust I stomp back into the palace. Barabbas is a notorious insurrectionist, a terrorist, and I am not about to release him. Not if I can help it....

Curtly I give the order for the prisoner they call Jesus to be taken away and scourged, trying not to think of what is in store for him.

I am troubled by Claudia's message. Although she is not a religious person, she does have what some call "second sight." She has been known to see things before they happen. It would not be wise to ignore her warning.

Pacing the marble floor of the palace, I search for a way to release this peasant without inciting the Jews to riot. Reports of political unrest in Judaea must not reach the ear of Caesar. If they do, I will not have to worry about a transfer. My career in the foreign service will be finished.

There is more to this case than meets the eye, of that I am certain. Even if this Jesus were guilty of tax evasion and subversive activities against Rome, that would be of little or no concern to Caiaphas. If only I knew the real reason for the Sanhedrin's involvement.

Hearing footsteps approaching, I turn and find myself confronted by a tragic figure. Our troublesome peasant has become a kind of clown king. Not only has he been scourged, leaving his bleeding back a mutilated mass of raw flesh, but the soldiers have also thrown a ragged robe of royal purple over his shoulder. For his head they have fashioned a crown of cruel Judeaen thorns.

> IN MY HANDS I HOLD THE POWER OF LIFE AND DEATH. YET IT FEELS AS IF I AM ON TRIAL HERE AND NOT HE!

I am tempted to laugh, so ridiculous does he appear, but something in his eyes stops me. By now he should be a broken man, humbled by the might of Rome. Or if not humbled, he should be defiant, consumed with a hate-filled rage.

He is neither.

Instead, there is about him a sense of destiny that is deeply disturbing.

I am the Roman governor, and he a mere peasant. In my hands I hold the power of life and death. Yet it feels as if I am on trial here and not he! Somehow I feel as if I am being weighed in the balances and found wanting.

More determined than ever to release him, I take him by the arm and walk outside to face the restless crowd. At the sight of us a hush falls over the street, and for a moment I am hopeful. Surely they can see that this beaten man is harmless, not deserving of death.

In a loud voice I shout, "Behold the man!"

I feel their rage almost before I hear it. "Crucify him!" they scream. "Crucify him!"

Their words strike me like physical blows, and for a moment I reel in stunned disbelief.

"But he is innocent," I fume. "He has done nothing worthy of death! Rome does not crucify petty thieves or so-called holy men. The cross is reserved for slaves and revolutionaries."[6]

47

"By our law he deserves death. He claims to be the Son of God, and for that he must die."

A god! I think, aghast. Could I, a mere mortal, have been playing judge to a god?

> HE IS A GOD, OF THAT I AM SURE.

The thought of it strikes fear in my heart. My throat closes and my breath comes in ragged gasps. In an instant Claudia's dream is made clear to me. But what can I do? I am a pawn in the hands of these mad Jews! They have trapped me between the wrath of Caesar and the vengeance of the gods.

Taking Jesus by the arm I escort him inside the palace where I confront him once more. "Where do you come from?" I demand, desperate to know the truth.

He does not answer, and my fear gives birth to angry rantings. "Why do you refuse to answer me? Don't you realize I have the power to crucify you or to set you free?"

"The only power you have over me," he says, regarding

me as a patient parent might an unruly child, "is what has been given to you by my Father."

He is a god, of that I am sure.

Mustering my courage I motion to Jesus to follow me onto the balcony. "This man is innocent," I declare in my most judicial voice. "I will now set him free."

They are not intimidated. With one voice they shout: "How dare you release a known enemy of Caesar!"

And again: "If you let this man go, you are no friend of Caesar!"

I cannot release him, that much is clear, but perhaps I can save myself. There must be a way I can make these Jews fully responsible for what happens to him.

Gesturing toward Jesus, who stands before me barefoot and bleeding, I say to the crowd, "Here is your king!"

In their rage they are like mad dogs. Shaking their fists and hissing, they shout, "Crucify him! Crucify him!"

"What?" I cry in mock amazement. "Crucify your king?"

T H E   G O V E R N O R

"We have no king but Caesar!" shout the chief priests, just as I knew they would.[7]

I've played this out about as far as I dare. Emotions are running high, and the slightest thing could start a riot. Calling for a basin of water, I make a show of washing my hands before the crowd. "I am innocent of this man's blood," I tell them. "It is your responsibility!"[8]

For a moment there is only stunned silence. Then they realize they have won. They have bent me to their will. Far back in the crowd a single voice shouts out: "Let his blood be on us and on our children!"[9]

> TOO LATE, I REALIZE THAT IN SAVING MYSELF I HAVE BETRAYED MYSELF.

He repeats it, and his voice is joined by another, and then another, until the whole crowd is shouting: "Let his blood be on us and on our children!"[10]

Wiping my hands on my tunic, I motion for the guard to lead Jesus away. At the door he pauses and looks long at me. Although I see nothing in his eyes but a sorrowful love, I feel sick. Too late, I realize that in saving myself I have betrayed myself.

For further study, see Life Lessons from Chapter Three.

The Acquitted

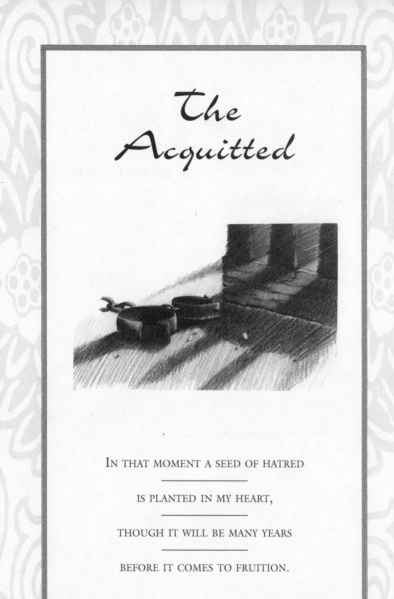

IN THAT MOMENT A SEED OF HATRED

_____

IS PLANTED IN MY HEART,

_____

THOUGH IT WILL BE MANY YEARS

_____

BEFORE IT COMES TO FRUITION.

CHAPTER FOUR

It is early, just after sunrise, but already I am awake, and thankfully too for it has been a miserable night. I slept fitfully, terrorized by all-too-real dreams, which made sleep a fearful venture at best.

With an effort I turn my attention to memories of a better time. For a moment I am a boy again, roaming the hillsides of Judea. Then I am sharing the Passover, in this very city, with my family. And now, as at other times, comes the memory that defines my life.

It is unbidden and unwelcome, but still it comes, even after all these years. My mother is weeping, and my father cannot speak. The Romans have killed my brother, the firstborn in our family. In that moment a seed of hatred is planted in my heart, though it will be many years before it comes to fruition.

The Romans say I am an insurrectionist, and I suppose they are right, though I've never wanted to believe that. I've always thought of myself as a patriot, what some people call a zealot — a man who is willing to die for the freedom of his nation.

In my younger years that may have been true. But somewhere along the way I changed. Hate replaced love, and I began to talk of killing rather than dying. Then I began to kill. First it was just the hated Romans. Then it was the collaborators — tax collectors and such like. Then it was anyone who got in my way.

In the process I learned a bitter truth. Every time I killed, a part of me died, a part that was good and decent. After awhile all that remained was the killing part. What I did and what I became were one and the same. The man who killed was now a killer — what the Romans call a revolutionist.

For awhile I believed I was doing it to avenge my brother. Perhaps it began that way, but soon I killed because that is what I am — a killer!

> TOO LATE I HAVE DISCOVERED THAT YOU CANNOT DESTROY A MONSTER WITHOUT BECOMING ONE YOURSELF.

The first time I took a Roman life it made me sick, but I soon got over it. Then I began to relish it, and finally I needed it. I was consumed with a lust for blood, not necessarily Roman either. As I near the end of my life I realize I have become the very thing I set out to destroy. Too late I have discovered that you cannot destroy a monster without becoming one yourself.

In the distance a guard barks an order jerking me from my melancholy thoughts. Then I hear the sound of a key grating in the lock. Finally a cell door swings open, groaning as it turns on its rusty hinges. I watch in the dim light as a fellow prisoner is chained and led away. He tries to be brave, but there is more than a hint of fear in his eyes, the kind of look I've seen in the eyes of trapped animals.

Shortly the guards return and the scene is repeated. Same sounds. Same pseudo courage. Same sick fear. With cold finality the cell door slams shut, and another prisoner is led away to die at the hands of the hated Romans.

T H E   A C Q U I T T E D

Finally, I am the only one left and then the guards return for me. Brusquely they order me from my cell and for a moment I am tempted to leap upon them. Resisting the impulse, I smile grimly and I extend my hands to receive the manacles.

To my amazement the guard simply turns away. "You're free," he snarls. "The governor has given you a pardon. Someone else is going to die in your place."

I am stunned. I cannot believe my ears. This is too good to be true! For just a moment I stand there, staring dumbly at their retreating backs. Then I burst into a fit of manic laughter. Running and jumping like a mad man, I shout, "I'm free! I'm free! I'm not going to die!"

> "YOU'RE FREE,"
> HE SNARLS.
> "THE GOVERNOR
> HAS GIVEN YOU
> A PARDON.
> SOMEONE ELSE IS
> GOING TO DIE IN
> YOUR PLACE."

Pushing by the surly guards, I stagger up the steep stairs and into the morning light. Even at this early hour the streets are jammed with people, and I allow the flow of the crowd to carry me along. Turning to a man on my left, I ask, "Does anyone know where we're going?"

Giving me a disgusted look, he says, "To the place called the Skull. There's going to be a crucifixion."

That being the last place I want to go, I work my way to the edge of the crowd. Escaping into a side street I soon lose my way in a maze of narrow, twisting streets. It doesn't matter. I am free, and my eyes drink in the colorful sights like a thirsty man gulping cool water.

The taste of freedom is on my tongue, the smell of freedom is in my nostrils. I'm alive, and once more a fit of laughter seizes me. I dance through the early morning crowd kissing strangers at random.

As fate would have it, I emerge on the Via Dolorosa just in time to see the mob making its way up the hill toward me. Once more I turn to go, but something holds me back. A morbid curiosity, I suppose, to see the one who will die in my place. Catching sight of a narrow staircase, I climb halfway up to get a better view. Soon I am joined on the stairs by the shop's proprietor.

> AT LAST HE SPEAKS, AND THOUGH HIS VOICE IS RAW WITH PAIN, HIS WORDS ARE TENDER, FILLED BOTH WITH COMPASSION AND FOREBODING.

Front and center I see my compatriots, each bearing the cross upon which he will die. Several paces behind them is a third man, so badly beaten as to be nearly unrecognizable. He too is carrying a cross. My cross. The one upon which I was supposed to die.

As I watch, he staggers a few steps and then falls, the weight of the cross pinning him to the pavement. Instantly a Roman whip bites into his bloody back. Involuntarily, I cringe. Even from this distance I can hear the sodden splat of hard leather burying itself in raw flesh. The prisoner is tough, I'll give him that. He doesn't utter a sound, not even so much as a groan.

Finally, he makes it to his knees before falling back a second time, and not even the threat of that deadly whip can empower him to rise again. Angrily, a soldier grabs the nearest bystander and orders him to carry the fallen man's cross. A good thing too, because anyone can see he is in no condition to carry it himself.

From the crowd a weeping woman runs to him, helps him to his feet, then quickly disappears back into the throng of onlookers. Staggering from pain and loss of blood, he allows his eyes to roam over the sea of faces, searching, I think, for the woman. At last he speaks, and though his voice is raw with pain, his words are tender, filled both with compassion and foreboding.

"Daughters of Jerusalem, do not weep for me; weep for yourselves and for your children. For the time will come when you will say, 'Blessed are the barren women, the wombs that never bore and the breasts that never nursed!' Then they will say to the mountains, 'Fall on us!' and to the hills, 'Cover us!'"[1]

THE ACQUITTED

An impatient soldier screams an order. Another cracks his deadly whip. Without further delay the death march is resumed.

What, I wonder, did *he* do to suffer such inhuman treatment at the hands of the Romans? My compatriots are revolutionaries and murderers as I am, yet neither of them was beaten. No doubt he is a most dangerous man. An assassin most likely, and guilty of ending the worthless life of some Roman dignitary.

IT'S THE LAST PLACE I WANT TO BE, BUT I AM GRIPPED WITH A COMPELLING CURIOSITY ABOUT THIS ONE WHO WILL DIE IN MY PLACE.

Turning to the proprietor I ask, "What do you know about that one?"

Following my gaze, he studies the abused prisoner for a moment before replying. "That's Jesus of Nazareth. He's a prophet."

"What did he do?"

"Nothing worthy of death, I can assure you. I've heard it said he healed sick folk and forgave sins. Things like that.

Someone said he even claimed to be the Son of God."

The condemned men are now in the street directly below me, and I hurry down the stairs and push my way into the crowd. It's the last place I want to be, but I am gripped with a compelling curiosity about this one who will die in my place.

After one final ascent we arrive at The Place of the Skull and the executions begin. Hard Roman hands hurl the prisoners down. Heavy hammers strike huge spikes, splintering flesh and bone. Blood splatters. Women weep. The mob goes mad.

Instinctively I sense there is more happening here than meets the eye, but for the life of me I can't figure it out. Watching him suffer I am haunted by a single thought: *That should be me. That cross was meant for me.*

After a time the light begins to fade, and I make my way down the hill and turn toward the city. There is no laughter now, no exuberant dancing in the streets, no kissing of strangers — just the taste of death upon my tongue. His death.

I wander aimlessly through the narrow, twisting streets, fleeing from the kaleidoscopic memories that now haunt me. Foremost among them is the stark image of his abused body spread-eagle on that Roman cross. Grateful though I am to be alive, I cannot escape the lingering guilt. Somehow it doesn't seem right that I should live while he dies in my place.

For further study, see Life Lessons from Chapter Four.

The Cyrenian

...A HEAVY HAND FALLS

UPON MY SHOULDER, AND I

AM ORDERED INTO THE STREET.

CHAPTER FIVE

pproaching the city via the north-south Samaria-Jerusalem road, I cannot avoid seeing the place of execution. It is situated on a bare rocky hill in a small triangle, formed where the road converges with the Joppa-Jerusalem road. From a distance it looks remarkably like a bleached skull as it rises fifteen or twenty feet above the surrounding terrain.

Today it is devoid of victims, a fact I note with no little gratitude. Nonetheless, it casts an ominous shadow across the road as I turn toward the Gennath Gate which leads into the city. My sons, Alexander and Rufus, are with me, and they stare in morbid fascination at the three cypress posts which stand like daggers stabbed in the crown of the skull. These are the uprights upon which the cross beams are attached to form the implements of execution. They are permanent, serving as a constant reminder of Roman justice, which is both swift and cruel.

Anxious as I am to put that grisly scene behind us, my

progress is slowed by the throng of pilgrims who are flooding into the city for the Passover. For us Hebrews it is the holiest of all feasts, commemorating our deliverance from Egypt.

Jerusalem, I observe, is alive with anticipation. There are people everywhere. The noise is constant — the cries of street vendors hawking their wares, shouted greetings between old friends, the running laughter of children, the bleating of sheep, and the cooing of doves. For me, the noise is nostalgic, resurrecting long-dead memories of a happier time.

FOR ME, THE NOISE IS NOSTALGIC, RESURRECTING LONG-DEAD MEMORIES OF A HAPPIER TIME.

As a boy I journeyed with my parents each year to this very city to celebrate my faith. Then, against their wishes, I married a Greek girl from Cyrene, a cultured city on the northern coast of Africa. Following the wedding, her father invited me to become part of the family's prosperous import business, and I accepted his offer.

Financially it was a good move, but it has not been without its drawbacks. For instance, my children are more Greek than Hebrew. They know almost nothing of their Jewish roots and have never celebrated Passover in the Holy City. Although their mother did not forbid it, she made her wishes clear enough.

In many ways ours is a good marriage, but on the issue of religion we have not been able to agree. She finds my Jewish faith barbaric with its blood sacrifices, not to mention sectarian. I, in turn, cannot stomach the proliferation of gods which her Greek tradition espouses. This year I have risked the peace of our house to celebrate Passover with my sons in the Holy City.

The crowds have stalled and, being a big man, I impatiently shoulder my way through, motioning for the boys to keep up. The side street upon which we are traveling twists around a corner and empties into the Via Dolorosa, where we are brought to an abrupt halt. The scene before me turns my stomach, and I frantically attempt to retrace my steps. My sons must not see this. It will spoil the whole Passover experience, taint every memory.

Too late I see Rufus and Alexander push through to the front of the crowd. In an instant their ruddy faces turn chalk white. For a moment their eyes are riveted on the drama being played out in the street before them, then they look around wildly, searching the crowd for me. Before I can push through the throng to them, a heavy hand falls upon my shoulder, and I am ordered into the street. This cannot be happening! I am a respected merchant, a well-placed man in the city of Cyrene. How dare these barbaric Romans cause me to defile myself by participating in the execution of these terrorists!

HOW DARE THESE BARBARIC ROMANS CAUSE ME TO DEFILE MYSELF BY PARTICIPATING IN THE EXECUTION OF THESE TERRORISTS!

But dare they do and I am powerless to refuse. At the centurion's order I grudgingly shoulder the fallen man's cross and fall in behind him. Shame burns my face and I am thankful the mother of my children is not here to endure this ignominy. Bad enough that my sons should see their father marched through the city in the company of common criminals!

As we move out, I study the men in front of me. At the head of the column is the centurion astride a gray horse. With controlled forcefulness he clears the street of the curious peasants, making way for the condemned men who follow bearing their crosses.

The man whose cross I carry brings up the rear and with each step he lags farther behind. It is not the fear of death that slows his pace, but the weakness of his abused body. He has been scourged, what the Romans call the "halfway death."[1] It is not supposed to be administered in addition to other punishment, but in his case it has been.

From time to time, I glance over my shoulder to make sure Rufus and Alexander are part of the crowd which follows our pathetic parade. I would like to send them away in order to spare them this scandalous trauma, but we are strangers in the city and I have no place to send them. It is better, I decide, for them to endure this gruesome experience than for us to risk becoming separated from each other.

> HIS HEAD IS BOWED, HIS BREATHING LABORED, HIS FACE A SUFFERING MASK.

Having settled that issue, I turn my attention to the task at hand. We are now ascending the steep hill leading to the Gennath Gate, and I am laboring beneath the weight of the cross. Though I am a large man and well muscled, it has been years since I have done physical labor, leaving me in no condition for this strenuous climb. Before we have reached the half-way point, my garments are soaked with sweat and my lungs are on fire.

Ahead of me the beaten man stumbles, and I think he must surely collapse, but somehow he finds the strength to go on. His head is bowed, his breathing labored, his face a suffering mask.

Behind me I hear the sound of sobbing. Not a wail but a whimper, and more sorrowful for it. It is coming from a small group of women who seem oblivious to everything except the bleeding man who staggers up the hill toward the place of his death. From the crowd I hear someone say, "It's Mary, his mother. Poor woman."

At last we reach the crown of the skull. Dropping his cross I fall to one knee, fighting to catch my breath. The sun is merciless, and I would give almost anything for a little shade and a drink of cold water.

Hardly has that thought taken shape in my mind before a shadow falls across my face, shielding me from the glare. Glancing up, I find myself looking full into his face.

My first impulse is to turn away in revulsion, so abused is his visage. One eye is swollen nearly shut, and beneath the bruises his skin is pasty and white. His beard is matted with dried blood, and flecks of spittle coat his raw lips.

Around me things continue as before. The soldiers prepare for the execution. The trailing crowd forms a semicircle before the condemned men. A group of religious leaders stand apart from everyone else, waiting impatiently. The women still weep. But all of this seems to recede, leaving just the two of us alone on this barren hill.

Inside my head I hear the ancient words of the prophet Isaiah:

"He had no beauty or majesty to attract us to him, nothing in his appearance that we should desire him. He was despised and rejected by men, a man of sorrows, and familiar with suffering. Like one from whom men hide their faces he was despised, and we esteemed him not."[2]

While I am still puzzling over this passage, he puts his hand upon my shoulder. His touch is both a blessing and

> TRY AS I MAY THOUGH, I AM NEVER ABLE TO FORGET THIS DAY OR MORE ESPECIALLY THE JEWISH CARPENTER...

a benediction, causing me to tremble — not in revulsion, but in reverence.

Before I can speak a soldier shoves me out of the way, while two others grab the man called Jesus and position him on the cross. An order is given, and the heavy hammer falls. It strikes the five-inch spike with a resounding clang that rolls over the crowd like a death knell.

I walk away, never looking back. I have no stomach for this sort of thing. Try as I may though, I am never able to forget this day or more especially the Jewish carpenter who placed his work-hardened hand on my shoulder just before laying it on the cross to receive that Roman nail.

For further study, see Life Lessons from Chapter Five.

The Convicted

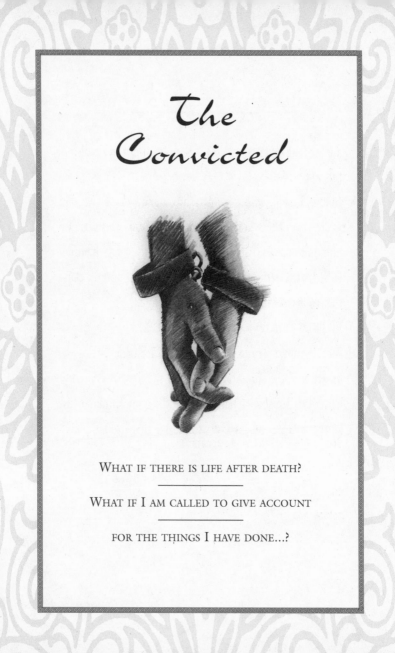

WHAT IF THERE IS LIFE AFTER DEATH?

WHAT IF I AM CALLED TO GIVE ACCOUNT

FOR THE THINGS I HAVE DONE...?

CHAPTER SIX

I hear the hollow cadence of the guards' tread and the clatter of armor as they approach my cell. To me it sounds like the angel of death. And well it might, for today is the day of my execution and they are coming for me. Now that my time is at hand, I find I am afraid. Not so much of dying, for I have grown weary with my life, but of being dead.

If I could be sure that death ended it all, I could go to my appointed hour bravely. But the uncertainty is unnerving. What if there is life after death? What if I am called to give account for the things I have done, for the sins I have committed?

Brusquely the guards order me from my cell, jerking me from my troubling thoughts. Slowly I move toward the door, carefully noting things I've never paid any mind to before: The way the early morning sun slants through the bars, casting long shadows on the near wall; dust motes suspended in the stream of light, delicate cobwebs in a dark corner.

Soon all of this will be just a fading memory, then when death comes I, too, will be just a memory. Bowing my head, I mumble a hasty prayer that I may be brave and that death may come quickly.

Momentarily I am filled with regret. It wasn't supposed to end like this. With painful clarity I recall the turning points in my life — those moments when I could have gone either way. Fleetingly I wonder what my life would have been like if I had chosen another path. There might have been a wife, perhaps even children. Though I have been mostly a homeless man, I now yearn for the comfort of hearth and family.

> MOMENTARILY I AM FILLED WITH REGRET. IT WASN'T SUPPOSED TO END LIKE THIS.

Thoughts of my misspent life weigh heavy upon me as the soldiers escort me out of the dungeon. Stepping into the street I am momentarily blinded by the morning light. It has been weeks since I have seen anything other than the inside of a Roman cell, and as my eyes adjust,

I marvel at the beauty of the holy city. The temple towers gleam against the bright blue of the sky, but it is the softer hues, the earth tones of the shops and houses, which catch my eye.

An order is given and two soldiers place a cross upon my shoulders as we prepare to march to the place of death. Looking around I see that I am one of three convicts who will be executed today for crimes against Rome. The routine is not unfamiliar to me. We will be paraded through the streets so the populace can see what happens to those who dare oppose Caesar. Then we will be crucified in a public place.

Of the other two men, one is a compatriot, while the second is a stranger. All I know about the second man is what I have gathered from the crowd. Apparently he is a prophet who claims to be king of the Jews — a serious offense in an empire where there is only one king, and that king is Caesar! From the looks of him, he has already had a taste of Roman justice — a bitter taste.

THE CONVICTED

From the head of the column the centurion barks an order and we move out. The pace is slow to accommodate the stumbling gait of the stranger, who has been beaten nearly to death. Neither my compatriot nor I have been scourged for which I am grateful. Although in the end, the brutal beating may prove to be a blessing hastening crucifixion's slow death.

AFTER A TORTUROUS CLIMB WE ARRIVE AT LAST AT THE PLACE OF THE SKULL.

After a torturous climb we arrive at last at The Place of the Skull. The vertical beams of the crosses have been permanently erected, and they now stand ominously against the Judeaen sky, a stark reminder of what is to come. I try to think of other things, like what a beautiful morning it is, as two Roman soldiers shove me down and pin my arms against the rough timber to receive the nails.

Obscenities spew from my compatriot's lips, and he spits at the soldiers who hold him in place. As the hammer falls, he screams in agony and empties his bowels. I turn my head so I do not have to see and pray that I may die with more dignity. I do not want to give these Romans the pleasure of seeing me cringe in either fear or pain.

I feel the spike heavy upon my flesh, and I will myself to be strong. The hammer descends, sending a flash of burning pain the length of my arm to explode in my head. Through gritted teeth I groan in spite of my determination not to. The same process is repeated with the other arm, then I am dragged to the vertical beam and hoisted up so my feet can be nailed.

For what seems a long time I hang there, drifting in and out of consciousness. Finally, through the yellow haze of my feverish pain, I hear the coarse joking of soldiers, followed by rowdy laughter. A bit later the soft sound of weeping again calls me back from the darkness. Looking down, I see an older woman, her face partially veiled. She stares at the stranger with a look that could only belong to a mother. I turn away, for I cannot bear the hurt I see in her eyes. It reminds me too much of what I saw in my mother's face. A suffering that only a son could put there. Even in my agony I find that I am fascinated by the stranger who hangs dying on the cross beside mine. Those who have come to see him suffer hate him with a fearful intensity; even as those who stand mute with grief revere him. As best I can gather, he claims to be the Son of God — an unlikely possibility, but one that takes hold of my mind and will not let go.

IS THAT WHAT THIS MAN IS DOING, SUFFERING FOR MY SINS?

How did the prophet put it when speaking of the Messiah? Something about bearing mankind's sin and making intercession for transgressors.[1]

Is that what this man is doing, suffering for my sins?

Another fragment of Scripture, learned in childhood then buried beneath years of hatred, now returns to my mind in the hour of death. The whole of it escapes me but the fragments are there — sheep going astray and the Lord laying on him all of our iniquity. Or perhaps it is people who stray like sheep.[2]

From a distance, as through a haze of pain, I hear my compatriot screaming in helplessness and rage: "You are the Christ, aren't you?" he shrieks. "So act like it! Save yourself and us!"[3]

"Aren't you afraid of God," I ask, my voice heavy with my own suffering, "considering you're about to die?"

Gathering my strength, I continue, "We are both getting what we deserve. But this man has committed no crime."[4]

He falls silent, and I cannot tell what he is thinking. As for me, my thoughts are racing. If this man really is the Son of God, then he holds my eternal destiny in his bleeding hands. A more rational part of my mind screams in protest. How can I think such a thing? He's only a man, as I am a man, and dying, as I am, at the hands of the hated Romans. Could such a broken piece of humanity be the Savior of mankind?

Reason says no.

Faith says yes!

Having made that leap, my mind now grapples with a new thought: *Why would the Son of God have time for the likes of me? What do I have to offer Him? A sordid past of hatred and bloodshed. A heart stained with sin. Nothing more, except my need.*

> IN AN INSTANT I AM FORGIVEN AND TRANSFORMED.

Still, faith finds its voice, and with trembling lips I call upon him. I do not ask for mercy, for that I do not deserve; nor for forgiveness, for to my way of thinking my sins must be past forgiving. No, all I dare to pray is, "Jesus, remember me when you come into your kingdom."[5]

And in response to my plea for a place in his thoughts he promises me a place in his kingdom!

"I tell you the truth," he says, "today you will be with me in paradise."[6]

In an instant I am forgiven and transformed. I am a new man![7] Although my hands and feet are nailed to a Roman cross, I am free, freer than I have ever been. I am dying, yet for the first time in my life, I am truly alive!

My strength is waning fast, and in the deepening shadows I sense the leering presence of death, yet I am no longer afraid. Moments ago I was facing death alone, now I share the promise of eternal life with the one whose dying is the defeat of death.

As the end draws near I cling more tightly to his promise, discovering as I do that death is no longer an enemy to be feared. My physical body may be dying, but my spirit is simply passing from one realm of life to another. Beyond the gloom I see a scarred hand reaching for mine and a familiar voice bids me come. In the light beyond I hear the sound of music and dancing.[8]

For further study, see Life Lessons from Chapter Six.

The Centurion

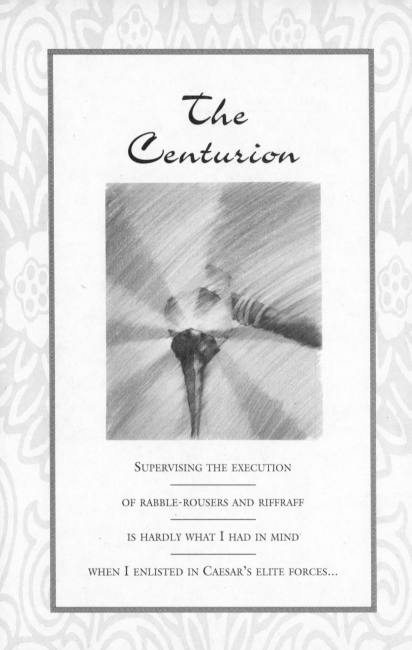

SUPERVISING THE EXECUTION

———

OF RABBLE-ROUSERS AND RIFFRAFF

———

IS HARDLY WHAT I HAD IN MIND

———

WHEN I ENLISTED IN CAESAR'S ELITE FORCES…

CHAPTER SEVEN

S upervising the execution of rabble-rousers and riffraff is hardly what I had in mind when I enlisted in Caesar's elite forces, yet more and more it falls my lot, especially since coming to this god-forsaken place. Judea is backward and arguably the worst posting in the Empire. It is inhabited by a rebellious people who seem determined to destroy themselves. On more than one occasion Pilate has been forced to order us to spill their blood. Unfortunately, even this show of military might has done little or nothing to change their ways.

Today I am overseeing the crucifixion of two robbers and the king of the Jews; at least that's what the sign for his cross says. JESUS OF NAZARETH, THE KING OF THE JEWS.[1] Apparently the governor wants everyone to know who he is, for the charge is written in three languages: Aramaic, Latin, and Greek.[2]

It's a good joke really, for he looks like no king I've ever seen. And his being from Nazareth is the best part. It's hardly the place of kings, being a frontier town on the southern border of Zebulun, known more for its crudeness than its royalty. Among the Jews there is a common saying: "Can anything good come out of Nazareth?"[3]

I hate this detail! I am a soldier, not an executioner. Still, I must admit that Rome has perfected the art of crucifixion. We adopted it from the Phoenicians, who were the first to use it. They preferred it to boiling in oil, impalement, stoning, strangulation, drowning, and burning, which all proved too swift for their taste. They wanted a form of execution that was as slow as it was painful, hence the cross.

> IT'S A GOOD JOKE REALLY, FOR HE LOOKS LIKE NO KING I'VE EVER SEEN.

In earlier times common soldiers served as executioners, but that proved so demoralizing to the troops that an official executioner is now assigned to each garrison. He nods to let me know the prisoners are in place and the crucifixion is ready to begin. Grimly I give the command and walk to the far side of the hill.

I am not squeamish, having shed more than my share of blood. But I have grown tired of this gruesome ritual. Though my back is turned, I see it all in my mind's eye. The cross beam is fitted beneath the prisoner's shoulders and his arms are extended along its length. Soldiers hold them in place while the executioner, with his right hand, probes the wrist for the little hollow spot where the so-called life line ends. Once he finds it, his movements are swift and sure. Taking a five-inch, square-cut iron nail from the apron around his waist, he positions it, then drives it through the hand and into the cross with a single blow. Moving to the other arm, he repeats the process.

Standing to his feet, he motions for the soldiers to lift the cross beam into place on the upright, which is already planted in the ground. A pair of soldiers grasp each side of the timber and lift it until the mortise can be fitted over the tenon, forming a cross.

Next the executioner kneels before the cross and, with the assistance of the soldiers, positions the prisoner's right foot on top of the left, being careful to make sure his legs are bent at the knee. With a measured blow he drives a third five-inch spike through both feet and into the hard wood.

Until now the condemned man has not uttered a sound, an unprecedented feat in the executioner's experience. Victims of crucifixion usually die raving like mad men. In extreme cases he has been known to cut out a man's tongue to silence him.

> **THERE IS ABOUT THIS SO-CALLED KING OF THE JEWS A CERTAIN DIGNITY...**

As he turns toward the next prisoner, the dying man finally speaks. Although dehydration has left his tongue as stiff as a stick, there is no mistaking his words. "Father," he cries, "forgive them, for they do not know what they are doing."[4]

His words take me by surprise and I turn to stare at him. There is something different about this crucifixion, of that I am sure. I can feel it. There is about this so-called king of the Jews a certain dignity, a sense of self, that neither beatings nor nudity can diminish.

Even the executioner senses it, and he pauses in his grisly ritual. Looking uncomfortable, he studies the man on the cross, while holding the implements of death in his hands. To his knowledge no one has ever prayed for him — not his abusing father, his whore of a mother, or anyone. At other crucifixions he has been cursed and reviled, even threatened, but never forgiven. Never before today.

A breath of a breeze brushes my hot skin, and a kind of hush falls over The Place of the Skull. From the edge of the crowd I hear someone say, almost reverently, "As a sheep before her shearers is silent, so he did not open his mouth."[5] With a grunt the executioner turns again to the second prisoner, who curses him loudly. Though he struggles mightily, it is no use, and in a matter of minutes he too is crucified. With equal dispatch the third prisoner is sent toward his death, and now there are three crosses silhouetted against the darkening sky.

Now comes the worst part — the waiting. It usually takes

several hours for even the weakest man to die. I do what men have always done — I lose myself in my work. According to Roman law, the effects of all condemned persons are confiscated by the State. Custom allows the soldiers assigned this duty to divide the spoils.

> LIKE RIVERS RUSHING TO THE SEA, MY ATTENTION RETURNS INEXORABLY TO THE CENTER CROSS AND THE MAN DYING THERE.

Accordingly, I toss a pair of well-worn sandals to one, to another a faded cloak. I continue this process until all that remains is the tunic belonging to the one called Jesus. It is an unusual garment, seamless and very expensive. Rather than tear it into pieces, to be divided among the soldiers, I decide they should cast lots for it.

As the soldiers gather around, I notice that the light seems to be fading, although it is not yet midday. Probably a figment of my imagination, I decide. Setting back on my heels I watch the soldiers roll the cubed bones, but soon I grow weary of their contrived frivolity. Once more I retreat to my solitary place on the edge of the hill.

Like rivers rushing to the sea, my attention returns inexorably to the center cross and the man dying there. With fatalistic fascination I watch as pain and exhaustion push him to the point of unconsciousness. His head lolls forward, causing his chin to rest against his chest. His entire weight now hangs on the nails in his hands, causing him excruciating pain, even as it forces his arms into a V position. From where I stand, I can see cramps knot the muscles in his arms and shoulders, causing him to twist in pain. Momentarily the pectoral muscles at the sides of his chest are paralyzed, making it impossible for him to breath. He can inhale, but he cannot exhale.

Frantically he raises himself on his wounded feet until his entire weight is supported by that single spike. With his shoulders now level with his hands, his breathing comes in ragged gasps. Desperately he fights the ghastly pain in his feet as long as he can, enduring severe cramps in his legs and thighs, in order to breathe for a moment more. When he can bear the searing pain no longer, his body sags against the spikes in his hands, and the whole excruciating process begins again.

Painful though the spike wounds are, they are never fatal, nor is the limited loss of blood that they cause. Death, when it comes, as inexorably it must, usually comes in the form of asphyxiation.[6]

Even a hardened witness such as myself can only bear so much, and I turn away to give my overwrought emotions a much needed reprieve. When I do, I cannot help but notice that it is much darker now, though the sun is nearly at its height. Glancing around, I see my fear mirrored on the faces of those who have lingered to await the end. We are a diverse

> SUDDENLY THE LITTLE LIGHT THAT IS LEFT IS SNUFFED OUT AND WE ARE PLUNGED INTO ABSOLUTE BLACKNESS.

group, made up of pagans and priests, weeping women and malicious mockers. Saint or sinner, it makes no difference now. In the deepening darkness fear stalks us all. Suddenly the little light that is left is snuffed out and we are plunged into absolute blackness. At first there is a mad cacophony of fear-infected screams, then only silence, except for the accusing voices within. A host of malignant memories set upon me. A hundred fingers point in accusation, a choir of discordant voices scream, "You are the one!"

How long this continues I do not know. Forever, it seems. Then there is absolute silence and the air is still, deathly still, as if nature itself were holding its breath. Deeper grows the darkness, pressing upon us like a physical weight. Then out of the darkness comes a haunting cry, hoarse and hurting.

"Eloi, Eloi, lama sabachthani?"[7]

There is no answer. Just his poignant question hanging in the darkness: "My God, my God, why have you forsaken me?"[8]

Beneath me the earth heaves and pitches, like the sea in the midst of a storm, driving me to my knees. Though my strength is nearly gone, something inside pushes me toward that center cross. On my hands and knees I inch forward, fumbling and feeling my way like a blind man.

After what seems an eternity I bump into it, my face rubbing hard against its course splinters. To my amazement I discover that the ground beneath the cross is solid, while all around it the earth continues to quake. In the darkness I feel his blood dripping upon me, and with it comes an inexplicable peace.

> TO MY AMAZEMENT I DISCOVER THAT THE GROUND BENEATH THE CROSS IS SOLID, WHILE ALL AROUND IT THE EARTH CONTINUES TO QUAKE.

How long I kneel there, embracing his cross, I do not know, but after a time the light begins to return, a little at first, then more. Glancing around, I notice that most of the onlookers are gone. The women remain huddled together, their eyes fixed on him. And at the far edge of the skull I see a large man with a grief-stricken face, a fisherman by the looks of him, though we are a long way from the sea. The women motion for him to join them, but he only withdraws deeper into himself.

Suddenly the silence and the half light are shattered by a shout. Jerking my head back, I look up. Somehow he has found the strength to push himself up to his full height. Filling his lungs with air he shouts, "It is finished."[9]

Though he is obviously dying, I know with absolute certainty that this is not the dying gasp of a helpless victim. What I have heard is the triumphant shout of a conquering king!

After a moment he speaks one last time, not as loud as before, but with unwavering conviction: "Father, into your hands I commit my spirit."[10]

One final breath whistles through his clinched teeth. Then his weight sags against the nails and he is still.

It makes no sense at all, but I am absolutely convinced he is who he claimed to be — God's Son. And now I lift my voice to join his. With all the reverence of which I am capable I give voice to the deepest conviction of my soul: "Surely this man was the Son of God!"[11]

For further study, see Life Lessons from Chapter Seven.

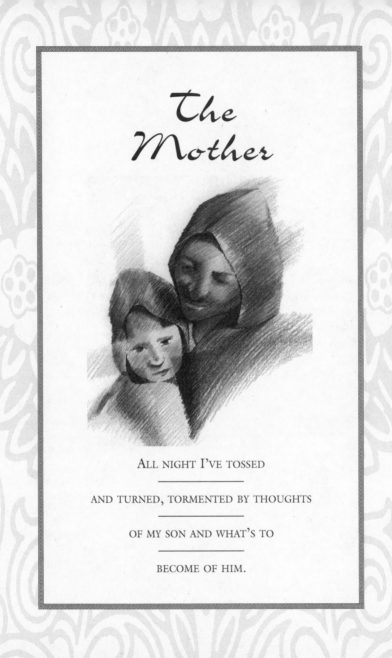

The Mother

ALL NIGHT I'VE TOSSED

———

AND TURNED, TORMENTED BY THOUGHTS

———

OF MY SON AND WHAT'S TO

———

BECOME OF HIM.

Opening the shutters I stare, with unseeing eyes, at the city shrouded in darkness below me. Morning is still a long way off, but I cannot bear to lie in bed a moment more. All night I've tossed and turned, tormented by thoughts of my son and what's to become of him. In my mind, I've replayed Simeon's fateful prophecy again and again.

Against my better judgment, I have allowed my sister Salome,[1] the mother of James and John, to persuade me to join her family in Jerusalem for the Passover. Secretly I hoped to see Jesus, though if the rumors I have heard are true, it would not be wise for him to risk making an appearance. Still, I hoped I might have a few minutes with him.

By the time I arrived, late Wednesday afternoon of Passover week, the city was wild with rumors. Jesus was reported to be here, but no one knows where. After entering the city in triumph on Sunday, he cleansed the temple on Monday, throwing out the money changers and driving out those who were selling. On Tuesday he dared to return to the temple to teach the people. And again early Wednesday he spoke, but then he disappeared — with good reason, for the chief priests are determined to put him to death.

We heard nothing all day Thursday, which was yesterday. I hope and pray he has slipped away, but in my heart I know it is not to be. The sword of which Simeon spoke is already doing its deadly work. With great effort I force myself to think of more pleasant things. Like the night my first-born son came into the world.

> I HOPE AND PRAY HE HAS SLIPPED AWAY, BUT IN MY HEART I KNOW IT IS NOT TO BE.

Behind me I hear the soft rustle of cloth. Turning from the window I discover Salome has entered my room. Placing her candle on a ledge she makes her way to me. Taking both of my hands in hers she says, "I saw your light and thought you might like some company."

She is such a dear sister. Always available, but never prying. Giving her a wan smile I say, "I was just thinking of the night Jesus was born."

"Please tell me about it," she says, drawing me out with her kindness.

"It's a long story," I warn her.

She just smiles and says, "We have the rest of the night."

Taking a deep breath I begin. "It wasn't a difficult birth as births go. Still, I didn't have anyone to help me except Joseph, and you know how helpless men can be at times like that. It's not the primitive stable or the bitter cold that I remember, or even my fear. All of that was forgotten as soon as I heard Jesus cry.

"There wasn't any water in the stable, so I used fresh straw to wipe him clean. Then I tore strips of cloth from a nearly new blanket and wrapped him in them. Joseph made a cradle of the manger, and we laid him there. I don't think I've ever been as happy as I was that night."

T H E   M O T H E R

Salome gives my hand a squeeze and nods knowingly, having given birth to children of her own.

"Forty days later, after the time of our purification according to the law of Moses,[2] we took Jesus to the temple to present him to the Lord. I wish we could have afforded a lamb, but all we could manage was two young pigeons. Still, I was so proud, especially when Simeon blessed him. He began to prophesy, and my blood ran cold. 'This child,' he said, 'is destined to cause the falling and rising of many in Israel.'[3]

> TURNING TO ME, HE LOOKED DEEP INTO MY EYES AND SAID, 'A SWORD WILL PIERCE YOUR OWN SOUL TOO.'

"Then came the words I've never been able to forget, words that I've lived with all these years. Turning to me, he looked deep into my eyes and said, 'A sword will pierce your own soul too.'[4]

"I asked Joseph what he thought Simeon meant, but he just shrugged it off. 'The irrational ramblings of a senile old man' was his conclusion. I knew better, and it wasn't long until my fearful premonitions proved correct.

"Jesus was barely two years old when King Herod ordered all the boys his age and under in Bethlehem and the surrounding area to be put to death.[5]

"When I learned of this evil decree, I was sick with fear. The nights were the worst. Sleep would not come, and when it did, I was tormented with terrifying dreams in which baby Jesus was torn from my arms and killed. More than once I awoke screaming, bathed in a cold sweat, the taste of fear bitter in my mouth.

"Joseph did what he could, but I would not be comforted, not as long as Jesus was in danger. Thankfully, God intervened. The angel of the Lord appeared to Joseph in a dream. 'Get up,' he said. 'Take the child and his mother and escape to Egypt.'[6]

"Though we fled Bethlehem that very night, it was years before I felt safe, really safe. Even in Egypt, fear was a part of every day.

"As you might guess, I became something of an overly protective mother. I wouldn't let Jesus out of my sight. I hovered over him, treasuring every smile, every slobbery kiss, hiding them in my heart against that terrible day when he would be taken from me.

FOR A LONG TIME HE HELD ME, AND NO MOTHER WAS EVER MORE LOVED.

"It was to be many years before my fears were fully realized. There were even times when I could almost forget that fateful prophecy, so ordinary did life seem. Jesus was good with his hands and seemed at home in the carpentry shop. Still, I knew it could not last, and as the years went by I sensed a growing restlessness in him. With increasing frequency I caught him staring off in the distance with a faraway look in his eye.

"One evening, just weeks before he turned thirty, I was returning from the well, where I had gone to draw water, when I saw him emerge from his shop. Turning toward the west, he wearily stretched his arms wide, casting the shadow of a cross on the wall behind him. In that instant Simeon's sword pierced my heart afresh. I knew that Jesus was going to die, and I knew the way he would die. Don't ask me how. Perhaps it was prophetic insight, or maybe a mother's intuition, but I knew.

"I remember the day he left Nazareth as clearly as if it were yesterday. He got work started in the shop, and then he came to me. He didn't say anything. What was there to say? For a long time he held me, and no mother was ever more loved. Then he was gone, without a backward look.

"For awhile we didn't hear anything. Then news began to filter back. John, our cousin Elizabeth's son, the one people called the Baptist, had declared that Jesus was 'the Lamb of God, who takes away the sin of the world!'[7]

"Sometime later a peddler brought news of Jesus' baptism. He witnessed it with his own eyes. According to his account he saw the Holy Spirit descended on Jesus in the form of a dove when Jesus emerged from the water. At the same time a voice from heaven said: 'You are my Son, whom I love; with you I am well pleased.'[8]

"For several weeks we didn't hear anything more. Later we learned that Jesus had fasted and prayed for forty days while doing battle with the tempter in the wilderness. Then he returned to Nazareth, and never was a mother more proud. When he stood up in the synagogue to read on the Sabbath, I thought my heart would burst with joy. He read so well. His voice was so rich, so resonant. 'The Spirit of the Lord is on me,'[9] he read. His voice brought the words of the ancient prophet to life.

"Finally he finished the passage and rolled up the scroll. Returning it to the attendant, he sat down. Every eye was upon him, and the room was tense with anticipation.

> WHEN HE STOOD UP IN THE SYNAGOGUE TO READ ON THE SABBATH, I THOUGHT MY HEART WOULD BURST WITH JOY.

'Today,' he said, 'this scripture is fulfilled in your hearing.'[10]

"That was too much. To the people's way of thinking, it bordered on blasphemy. Angrily they asked each other, 'Isn't this the carpenter? Isn't this Mary's son and the brother of James, Joseph, Judas, and Simon? Aren't his sisters here with us?'[11]

"Seizing him, they dragged him out of the synagogue and to the brow of the hill on which the town was built. They had every intention of hurling him off the cliff to his death, but he walked right through the crowd and no man laid a hand on him.[12] It was the most uncanny thing I've ever seen. Still, my relief was short-lived. Seeing their anger, I knew it was only a matter of time until they killed him."

Pressing my lips together, I close my eyes. A tear escapes from the corner of my eye leaving wet tracks down my cheek. Quickly I wipe it away and force myself to give Salome a brave smile. She returns my smile and her eyes tell me she understands.

"That's the last time Jesus came home. From that day he lived in Capernaum.[13] He lived there, I believe, to spare me. He knew how I suffered when people attacked him, especially the religious leaders.

"But we cannot escape our destiny, and the sword of which Simeon spoke is mine. It will only be a matter of time until it pierces my soul to the hilt."

> WE ARE STANDING DIRECTLY UNDER THE GOVERNOR'S BALCONY WHEN HE LEADS JESUS OUT. AT THE SIGHT OF HIM I NEARLY FAINT.

We sit for sometime in silence, each of us immersed in our own thoughts. I sense that Salome would like to comfort me, but she is too wise to give me false assurances. And like me, she is aware of the grave danger Jesus is in.

Together we watch as the sun rises, slowly washing the darkness from the city below.

Suddenly our solitude is interrupted by a frantic pounding at the door.

It is John, Salome's youngest son, and he brings the worst possible news. Jesus has been arrested and is being taken to Pilate, the Roman governor. Frantically we fling on our clothes and follow John through the winding streets toward the governor's palace.

By the time we arrive, a crowd has gathered and their mood is ugly. Working our way through the mass of people, we manage to position ourselves near the front. We are standing directly under the governor's balcony when he leads Jesus out. At the sight of him I nearly faint. "What have they done to him?" I cry, unable to tear my eyes from his mutilated face. His lips are a bloody pulp, one eye is swollen completely shut, and his back is ripped to raw shreds — the work of a Roman whip. On his head, thrust far down, is a cruel crown of three-inch Judeaen thorns. A discarded robe of royal purple is carelessly thrown about his shoulders, making the mockery complete.

Motioning for the crowd to be silent, Pilate says, "Here is your king."[14]

THE MOTHER

At that the mob goes mad. "Crucify him!" they scream, "Crucify him!"

"Shall I crucify your king?" he asks.

As with one voice they shout, "We have no king but Caesar."[15]

> JOHN COVERS MY HEAD WITH HIS ARMS, BUT THERE IS NO WAY TO SHUT OUT THE MADNESS.

Seeing he cannot prevail, Pilate yields to their will and orders Jesus put to death. We watch in stunned disbelief as the soldiers lead him away.

Numbly we follow them up the Via Dolorosa, and out the city gates to a skull-shaped hill called Golgotha. There they crucify him. They strip him and nail him to a cross. As the executioner swings his heavy hammer, I turn away in revulsion, burying my face in John's chest while spasms of grief rack my tortured soul.

John covers my head with his arms, but there is no way to shut out the madness. Shouted orders from the soldiers mingle with the tortured screams of the condemned, and are joined in the fearful din by the grief-stricken wails of family and friends.

Worst of all are the taunts of the religious leaders. "He saved others," they sneer. "Let him save himself if he is the Christ of God, the Chosen One."[16]

Others mock him saying, "You who are going to destroy the temple and build it in three days, come down from the cross and save yourself!...Let this Christ, this King of Israel, come down now from the cross, that we may see and believe."[17]

Such cruelty, such hatred, I have never seen. It is as if hell itself has erupted and is spewing its poisonous venom over the earth. Then, in the midst of that cesspool of hatred, I hear the sound of love!

"Father...."

His voice is raspy, hardly recognizable at all.

"Father, forgive them, for they do not know what they are doing."[18]

His words are no more than a ragged whisper, but there is no mistaking them. To my knowledge, no one but Jesus dares call God "Father."

Like a magnet his voice draws me. Turning my face from John's chest I look full at my firstborn son. When I do, the sword of which Simeon spoke pierces my soul anew. My grief and sorrow are unbearable, yet there is something else too. A wordless hope, an inner conviction too intangible to be defined, yet too real to be denied.

> SOMEHOW I KNOW THAT HE IS NOT A HELPLESS CAPTIVE, BUT A WILLING SACRIFICE.

Somehow I know that he is not a helpless captive, but a willing sacrifice. In a way I cannot explain, I truly understand that his execution is not simply a miscarriage of human justice, but the just decree of a holy God. For this reason was he born. He is the Lamb of God, doing what he came to do, suffering for the sins of the world.

Caiaphas, Pilate, the Roman soldiers, even the blood-thirsty mob, are not his executioners. They are mere instruments in the hand of God. This crucifixion is God's doing — a terrible but vital part of His eternal plan.

Knowing this does not make my grief any less, but it does give me the strength to bear it. Now I want to encourage Jesus. I want to let him know I understand what he is doing, that I support him.

Breaking away from John, I run to the foot of the cross where he can see me. Looking down, his gaze finds me, and for a moment we hold each other with our eyes. I feel John put his arm around me, but I cannot tear my eyes away from Jesus.

"Dear woman," he says, and there is so much love, so much compassion in his words, I think my heart will break. *How can he think of me at a time like this,* I ask myself. Then his eyes shift to John, and he says, "Here is your son."[19] And to John he says, "Here is your mother."[20] Something must have passed between them then, some unspoken message perhaps, because John takes my arm and leads me away. I don't want to go; I can't bear to leave Jesus to die alone. Yet I know I can't stay. Jesus wants me to go. He wants to spare me the pain of watching him die, and I cannot deny him this final act of kindness.

The sky is growing dark as I descend from Golgotha and

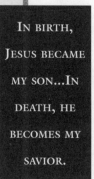

turn toward Jerusalem. John lets me lean on him as he leads me toward the home of my sister. A good thing too, for I am nearly blind with grief. Now that Simeon's sword has finally been revealed I find it is much worse than I could ever have imagined.

Still, I draw some small comfort from the knowledge that this is part of God's eternal plan. Turning to John I say, "In birth, Jesus became my son and I his mother. In death, he becomes my savior and, unworthy sinner though I am, I can now become a child of God. Through him I too can call God 'Father.'"

For further study, see Life Lessons from Chapter Eight.

IN BIRTH, JESUS BECAME MY SON...IN DEATH, HE BECOMES MY SAVIOR.

The Father

IN ETERNITY PAST, BEFORE

I LAID THE FOUNDATIONS

OF THE WORLD, I EMBRACED

THIS FATEFUL DAY.

CHAPTER NINE

In eternity past, before I laid the foundations of the world,[1] I embraced this fateful day. When the creation of man was just a distant thought, and his fall an unrealized tragedy, I committed Myself to redemption's plan. Still, now that the time has come, I find I am grievously pained at what must be done.

My heart is torn as Jesus pleads with Me. "Abba, Father," He says, "everything is possible for you. Take this cup from Me."[2]

It is all that I can do not to snatch that deadly cup from His trembling hands and hurl its toxic dregs into outer darkness. But what would that accomplish, beyond a momentary reprieve? In truth, it would only delay the inevitable. There is no other way.

His voice again, heavy with hurt, but trusting still. "Father, if it is possible, may this cup be taken from Me. Yet not as I will, but as You will."[3]

I nod toward the angel at My right hand and in an instant he is kneeling beside Jesus, strengthening Him.[4] By now

THE FATHER

My Son's sweat is like drops of blood falling to the ground.[5] His words tear at My heart, but there is nothing I can do.

"Abba, Father," He says "everything is possible for You..."[6] If only that were true!

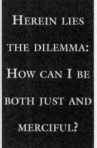

HEREIN LIES THE DILEMMA: HOW CAN I BE BOTH JUST AND MERCIFUL?

With a word I call worlds into existence. At My command darkness is turned into light and order comes out of chaos. I make the barren womb fruitful and give the childless children. I speak from a bush that burns but is not consumed. I turn rivers into blood and divide the sea so that My people may pass over on dry ground. By My Spirit the virgin conceives and the Son of God becomes the Son of Man, but I cannot grant Jesus' desperate plea.

Everything is possible for Me — everything, that is, except this!

Being absolutely just I cannot allow a single sin to go unpunished; nor can I forgive a solitary sinner until My justice is fully satisfied, until every sin — past, present, and future — is punished.

At the same time, I am also merciful and I cannot turn My back on Adam's lost race. If I were to do so I would betray that part of My eternal character. Because of Who I am, I am compelled to satisfy both My justice and My mercy.

Herein lies the dilemma: How can I be both just and merciful? How can I forgive Adam's sinful race without betraying the just demands of My holy nature? Moreover, how can I judge their sins without denying My love and mercy?

The cross is the only answer, for in the cross both My mercy and My justice will be fully vindicated. Through His sacrificial death, Jesus will manifest My unconditional love even as He suffers the full penalty for humanity's sins, thus satisfying the just demands of My righteous character. He speaks again, no longer pleading but submissive and obedient, "My Father, if it is not possible for this cup to be taken away unless I drink it, may Your will be done."[7]

THE FATHER

With trembling hands He takes the cup, drinks deeply of its deadly dregs, and the final act begins. From eternity I watch as redemption's drama unfolds. It is a script prepared in eternity past. I know its scenes well, having created them Myself — yet the stark reality of this dreadful moment rips at My heart.

> **NEVER HAS THERE BEEN ANYTHING LIKE THIS, NOT IN TIME OR ETERNITY.**

Now the executioner places a five-inch iron spike against the outstretched hand of My only begotten Son. As he raises his huge hammer I find myself longing for another way, a plan that would save both My beloved Son and Me from this awful hour. But in eternity there is only silence, for there is no other way, and there is no other sacrifice for the sins of Adam's race.

Finally, the tortured silence is shattered by the sound of a solitary hammer striking a nail, and Jesus is crucified. His life blood spills out as a ransom for lost men and women. He suffers the full penalty for Adam's sin.

Watching My beloved Son writhe in the agonies of crucifixion's slow death, I am torn with conflicting emotions. A part of Me longs to tear the darkness away, to gently lift His trembling body from the cross. Oh that I might end His sufferings, that I might bathe His wounds with My tears.

Yet, another part of Me is nearly in awe witnessing His sacrificial love. Never has there been anything like this, not in time or eternity.

As the sixth hour[8] approaches, darkness descends. In an act reminiscent of the day of atonement, I place My hands upon His bloodied head[9] and, in a voice only He can hear, I impute to Him all the sins of Adam's lost race.[10] In the deepening darkness My sinless Son becomes the greatest sinner in time or eternity.

During the three hours of light He suffered at the hands of wicked men. In the three hours of darkness He suffers at My holy hand. During the three hours of light He suffered man's injustice. In the three hours of darkness He suffers My divine justice. During the three hours of light He suffered as the innocent for the guilty. In the three hours of darkness He suffers not only as the condemned for sin, but as sin itself![11]

In order to reconcile the world to Myself, I must banish Jesus from My presence. He must suffer the full retribution for the sins of mankind. Therefore, with determined deliberateness I turn My back on Him. I abandon Him. This is the ultimate punishment: separation from My holy presence.

> ON THIS DAY WE WILL EACH SUFFER IN OUR OWN WAY. HE — JUDGMENT AT MY HAND, AND I — HIS HAUNTING CRY!

Though He bore the brutality of the Roman whip without a whimper and suffered the cruelty of the cross without uttering a word, this separation is more than He can bear in silence. Alone in the darkness, He screams, "My God, my God, why have You forsaken me?"[12]

I will Myself not to hear, but it is no use. There is no escaping His haunting cry. On this day We will each suffer in Our own way. He — judgment at My hand, and I — His haunting cry!

To see My Son suffer at the hands of sinful men was nearly more than I could bear, but it was nothing compared to this. Now I am the perpetrator of His pain, the source of His agony. I have smitten Him and afflicted His soul. I have crushed Him and laid upon Him the iniquity of all mankind. I have made His life an offering for sin. I have cut Him off from the land of the living, made Him pour out His soul unto death.[13] I have forsaken Him, inflicting a pain like no other. At My hands He has suffered the torments of the damned!

Finally it is over and in death He triumphs. Though I have not relented nor displayed even a hint of mercy toward Him, He still trusts me. With His dying breath He offers Me His soul.

And now I hear Him call My Name. "Father," he says "into Your hands I commit My spirit."[14]

It is finished!

THE FATHER

Sin's debt is finally paid, My holy justice fully satisfied. At last I am free to forgive every son and daughter of Adam! It makes no difference how far they may have fallen or the sinful deeds they may have done.

Only one thing remains and I now turn My attention to the temple in Jerusalem. Laying hold of the curtain, separating the holy place from the holy of holies where My presence abides, I tear it in two from top to bottom.[15] Never again will anything other than unbelief separate Me from Adam's race. Now and forever I am as near as the smallest prayer whispered in Jesus' name.

> AT LAST I AM FREE TO FORGIVE EVERY SON AND DAUGHTER OF ADAM!

Is there a man who has betrayed the trust of his children, sinned against their innocence?

Your debt is paid!

Is there a woman who has lost her virtue, a man who is trapped in sexual sin?

Your debt is paid!

Is there a son who has broken his mother's heart, a daughter who has forsaken the teachings of her youth?

Your debt is paid!

Is there a junkie, a dealer, a pimp, or a prostitute who has lost all hope?

Your debt is paid!

Is there a religious leader living a double life, a merchant trapped in crooked deals, a politician on the take?

Your debt is paid!

My Son, your Redeemer, paid it all.

"'Come now, let us reason together,' says the Lord.
'Though your sins are like scarlet,
they shall be white as snow;
though they are red as crimson,
they shall be like wool.'"[16]

For further study, see Life Lessons from Chapter Nine.

The Harlot[1]

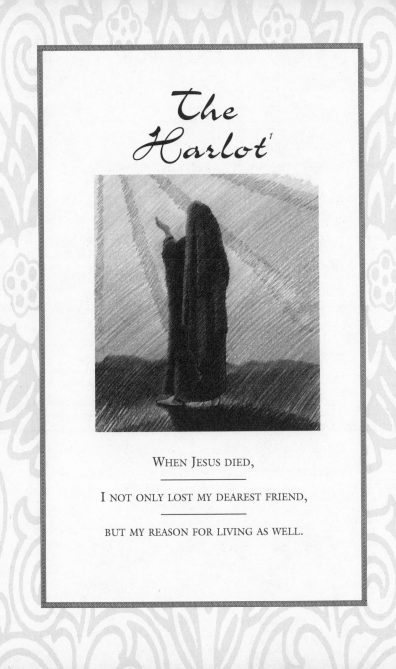

WHEN JESUS DIED,

———————

I NOT ONLY LOST MY DEAREST FRIEND,

———————

BUT MY REASON FOR LIVING AS WELL.

CHAPTER TEN

It is still dark as I slip out of the house and make my way toward the tomb where the one I love lies cold and still in death. I probably should have waited for the others, but the sleepless night seemed endless, and I could bear my tormenting thoughts no more. Besides, I need some time alone, some time to sort through my jumbled thoughts.

When Jesus died, I not only lost my dearest friend, but my reason for living as well.

Like Peter, I truly believed Jesus was "the Christ, the Son of the living God."[2] Now I don't know what to believe. As I watched him die two days ago, something died inside me. A black despair enveloped me and gave birth to an all too familiar hopelessness.

For two nights and a day I have wrestled with my tormenting thoughts, and I am no nearer to a resolution. Was Jesus just a man, an extraordinary man to be sure, but still nothing more than a man? His death seems to prove that beyond question. Yet, if he was only a man, how do I explain his miracles? More importantly, how do I explain what he did for me?

For years I existed in a nightmare world. I lived in the darkness inside of me with those who had taken residence there — malevolent spirits, abused and abusing. My name became a byword in the city of my birth — Mary, the mad whore of Magdala. The life I lived I hated, as I hated myself, but I was powerless to change. I was a prisoner, and death seemed my only escape.

> THE LIFE I LIVED I HATED, AS I HATED MYSELF, BUT I WAS POWERLESS TO CHANGE. I WAS A PRISONER, AND DEATH SEEMED MY ONLY ESCAPE.

Then one day he came, this itinerant holy man, the one they called Jesus. I waited until he was alone, and then I approached him, driven by the demons within. It was not his help I sought, but his destruction. With a well-deserved confidence I set out to make short work of this popular prophet.

Intuitively I knew he could not be approached as other men. With them I appealed to the weakness of their flesh, reducing them to puppets of their passion. He was different. His strength was his weakness. His compassion would be his undoing.

"Prophet," I called in a voice hardly more than a whisper, "have you a moment?"

Peering into the shadows where I stood, his eyes sought mine. It was as if he looked into my soul! Suddenly I felt naked. Ashamed. And a strange feeling it was for a woman such as I, a woman who had shamelessly sold her nude flesh to more men than she could remember.

He spoke a single word then: "Mary."

No man had ever called me by my name. Woman? Yes. Whore? More times than I would like to remember. Even sweetheart in the heat of passion. But never Mary.

Inside me the spirits were in a frenzy. "Flee!" they screamed. "It's a trap!"

As I turned to go he spoke my name again, and the darkness within eased just a little and then a bit more. Love washed over me, his love, and I found myself weeping. Almost without realizing what I was doing, I slipped out of the shadows and knelt at his feet. Reaching down he placed his hand on my head and said, "Be free!"

At his words the darkness was shattered, the spirits expelled![3]

Taking my hand, he drew me to my feet and looked deep into my eyes. "Daughter," he said, "your sins are forgiven."

IS GOD NOW DEAD? HAS EVIL TRIUMPHED OVER GOOD?

There was no shame then, nor fear — only love. A holy love, pure and clean. Gone was the madness within. Gone was my shame and sickness of soul. Gone was my brokenness and despair. Gone was all my sin, washed away in the light of his love!

If he was only a man, how do I explain that?

Yet, if he was indeed the Son of God as he claimed, what does his death mean? Is God now dead? Has evil triumphed over good?

The answers are beyond me. All I know is that Jesus is dead, and I might as well be also. I'm walking and breathing, but I'm no longer alive.

As I traverse the silent streets I find myself weeping again, or perhaps I should say still, for my tears have been endless. He is dead, and I am alone. All the tears in the world cannot change that, but still I weep. I weep, for in this awful moment that is all I have left of him, just my grief.

The first hint of day is coaxing the darkness from the eastern sky as I enter the garden. For just a moment I am disoriented. Things look so different in the dark, and the tomb I have found is empty. Carefully I retrace my steps, thinking I must have taken the wrong path. No. This is the right way, of that I am sure.

THE HARLOT

The tomb is empty! They have stolen the body of my Lord. Grief and rage nearly overwhelm me. Does the envy of the religious leaders know no limit? Wasn't it enough to kill him? Must they now desecrate his body as well?

I thought nothing could hurt me beyond the pain I had already suffered. I was wrong! Now I am suffering wounds to my wounds. Not only have they killed my Lord, but now they have robbed me of this small comfort as well.

> "THE BODY OF JESUS IS GONE, BUT IT COULD NOT HAVE BEEN TAKEN BY HUMAN HANDS OR THE GRAVE CLOTHES WOULD HAVE BEEN DISTURBED."

My grief is too great to bear alone. I must tell someone, someone who loved him as much as I did. Retracing my steps I hurry through the narrow streets in search of Peter. At last I find him, and John too. Between sobs I pour out the details of this new indignity. Like me they are outraged and insist on seeing the empty tomb for themselves.

Through the nearly empty streets they run, pausing occasionally to catch their breath. I follow at a distance, weighted down with despair.

By the time I reach the empty tomb, Peter and John have already examined it and are talking excitedly. Turning to me Peter says, "The body of Jesus is gone, but it could not have been taken by human hands or the grave clothes would have been disturbed."

"See for yourself," John says, motioning for me to enter the tomb. "The grave clothes are still here, but they have not been disturbed. No bandage is undone. None of the folds have been moved. They are just shrunken, empty."

It is obvious they are convinced that something supernatural has happened, but the subtleties of their arguments escape me. I do not care whether the grave clothes have been left behind or not. All that remains of the one I loved is gone. Not only is Jesus dead, but his body is missing as well.

Seeing that I will not be convinced, Peter and John leave me alone and return to the city. I want to believe, I really do, but it is more than I can manage. I cannot endure another disappointment. Already the darkness threatens to reclaim me, and I cling to my sanity by my fingernails.

> **WHAT GOOD ARE ANGELS WHEN MY LORD IS DEAD AND HIS BODY DESECRATED?**

Weeping disconsolately before the empty tomb, I remember the spices I prepared to anoint his body for burial. What will I do with them now? Such a small thing in view of the monumental events which have rocked me these last few days. Still I am undone. A fresh wave of grief seizes me, and I wonder why I have been denied even this final act of love.

In desperation I bend down to look into the empty tomb. Maybe I too can coax some ray of hope from the abandoned grave clothes. It's not likely, but still I try.

So great is my grief that the sight of two angels in white,

sitting where Jesus' body is supposed to be, hardly registers. What good are angels when my Lord is dead and his body desecrated? Dismissing them without a second thought I turn toward the garden.

Through my tears I see the form of a man approaching through the early morning shadows. Maybe he is the caretaker. Maybe he saw something! Maybe he knows where the body of Jesus is.[4]

"Sir!" I cry, not even attempting to disguise my grief, "If you know where they have taken the body of Jesus, please tell me, and I will get it."[5]

He answers me with a single word, a single word that dispels the darkness within. A single word that rescinds all of the madness of Friday. A single word that undoes all of the damage wrought by my grief. A single word that forever shatters the myth of death.

"Mary."[6]

Like the first time, love washes over me, and joy. Once more I know who I am: Mary Magdalene, beloved of the Father and the Son.

Not Mary, the mad whore of Magdala. Not Mary, the abused, the rejected, the dirty toy of even dirtier men. Not Mary, the habitation of demons. Not even Mary, the bereaved.

I CAN'T SEE HIM, BUT I HAVE THE STRONGEST SENSE THAT HE IS HERE, THAT HE WILL ALWAYS BE HERE...

With that single word, all sin and death have attempted to do and all hell's fury has threatened is undone.

I slowly turn toward him. *He's not dead,* I think in amazement. *Peter and John were right. He's alive!*

"Teacher!" I cry, falling before him, my heart undone.

I want to hold him and never let him go. Yet for all his tenderness there is about him a transcendent glory which precludes such contact.

"Go to my brothers," he instructs me, "and tell them I am returning to my Father and your Father, to my God and your God."[7]

And then he is gone — yet in a way I can't explain he isn't gone. I can't see him, but I have the strongest sense that he is here, that he will always be here, nearer than the breath I breathe and more alive than life itself.[8]

For further study, see Life Lessons from Chapter Ten.

The Doubter

UNLESS I SEE THE NAIL MARKS

———————

IN HIS HANDS...

———————

I WILL NOT BELIEVE.

CHAPTER ELEVEN

ight blankets the city and the streets are nearly deserted as I make my way toward the house of Mary the mother of Mark. It is a safe house and I am sure the disciples will be sequestered there behind locked doors. It is where we celebrated the Passover, in an upper room, on the night Jesus was betrayed. Was it only three days ago? It seems longer. So much has happened.

Once more I replay the tragic events in my mind. If only Jesus would have listened to me. I tried to warn him. My twin brother,[1] who is a merchant in Jerusalem and well connected, sent word telling me that the Sanhedrin had put a price on Jesus' head.[2] When I relayed his warning to Jesus he simply said, "The hour has come for the Son of Man to be glorified. I tell you the truth, unless a kernel of wheat falls to the ground and dies, it remains only a single seed. But if it dies, it produces many seeds."[3]

Seeing Jesus was determined to celebrate the Passover in Jerusalem regardless of the risk, we all resolved to go with him. Well do I remember saying, "Let us also go, that we may die with him."[4]

How empty those words now seem, in light of what happened in Gethsemane. When the temple guards came to arrest Jesus we showed our true colors. With the exception

WELL DO I REMEMBER SAYING, "LET US ALSO GO, THAT WE MAY DIE WITH HIM."

of Peter and John, we all fled. Cowards, each and every one of us. And a shamefaced lot we were when we finally regrouped at the home of Lazarus in Bethany.

We spent a sleepless night bickering among ourselves. Most of the disciples wanted to return to Galilee at first light, reasoning that Caiaphas would not pursue us there. James, the oldest son of Zebedee, said we could go if we wanted to, but he wasn't leaving without his brother. At last it was decided we would remain in Bethany until we could find out what had become of Jesus, as well as Peter and John. To my way of thinking, it was a foolish decision and not one I felt obligated to abide by. Any fool could figure out that the home of Lazarus was the first place Caiaphas would look if he was serious about finding us. It was widely known that Jesus raised Lazarus from the dead. Nor was it any secret that we had all enjoyed that good man's hospitality on numerous occasions.

Without telling the others what I was doing, I slipped away and made my way to the house of my brother. He was not a follower of Jesus and I reasoned no one would look for me there.

It was early when I arrived, just after daybreak, but already he was conferring with one of his contacts. I waited until the man left, then slipped into the house. Immediately my brother hustled me into his private quarters, being careful that none of the servants saw me.

Once we were alone he said, "Thank God you are safe. The Sanhedrin has found Jesus guilty of blasphemy and sentenced Him to die. Even now they are delivering Him to Governor Pilate to be crucified."

"What is to become of those of us who followed him?" I asked, fear making my words come out in a rush.

"It is too early to know," he replied, "but I do think it would be prudent for you to remain out of sight for a few days — at least until things settle down."

Rowdy laughter and the clatter of armor jerk me back to the present. Darting into an alley, I crouch in the deep shadows as two half drunk soldiers stagger up the street. Once they are out of sight I resume my journey, being careful to keep my mind on what I am doing. I take a circuitous route, doubling back several times to make certain I am not being followed. The last thing I want to do is lead a temple spy to Mary's house.

THE LAST THING I WANT TO DO IS LEAD A TEMPLE SPY TO MARY'S HOUSE.

The young man John Mark answers the door. When he recognizes me he shows me to the upper room, where I confront another locked door. For a moment I stand there collecting my thoughts. Through the door I can hear the murmur of voices and, from time to time, what sounds like joyous laughter. Puzzled, I hesitate, my hand half raised, poised to knock.

Suddenly the door is opened and I find myself face to face with John. For a moment we stare at each other, neither of us believing our eyes. John is not at all like I expected him to be. He should be beside himself with grief. Instead he is ecstatic with joy.

Grabbing me by the arm, he pulls me into the room shouting, "Thomas is here!"

Everyone is talking at once, and it is more than my grief-stricken mind can comprehend. As best I can gather, they are telling me that Jesus is not dead, but alive. They all claim to have seen Him, some of them more than once.

Peter notices my dazed expression and raises his hands for silence. Around me the room grows quiet. Now everyone is looking at me, waiting for my response. I want to believe, I truly do, but I can't. I'm at a loss to explain the transformation that has come over the rest of the disciples, but I am quite sure it has nothing to do with anything so far-fetched as a living Jesus.

Finally, I find my voice and blurt out, "Unless I see the nail marks in his hands and put my finger where the nails were, and put my hand into his side, I will not believe it."[5]

> PLOTTING A RESURRECTION HOAX·WAS THE LAST THING ON OUR MINDS.

Momentarily they are taken aback, but soon they return to their joyous fellowship. Obviously it will take more than my cynicism to dampen their newfound enthusiasm.

Cleopas breaks away from the group and comes to join me in the corner, where I sit apart from the others. After some small talk, he tries to tell me about his experience on the road to Emmaus,[6] but grows discouraged when I show no interest. After awhile, Mary Magdalene sits down beside me. Finding me no better company than Cleopas did, she too leaves me to brood alone.

I came here tonight to clear up a rumor that is circulating in Jerusalem. It is reported that the body of Jesus was stolen out of the tomb while the guards slept. According to my brother's sources, the disciples of Jesus are said to be responsible.[7]

When my brother reported this information to me, I snorted in disdain. "The last time I saw my fellow disciples," I explained, "we were thinking of nothing but saving our own skins. We were shattered by the sudden turn of events and reeling at the death of Jesus. Plotting a resurrection hoax was the last thing on our minds. If we weren't willing to risk our lives to rescue Jesus when he was arrested in Gethsemane, why would we now risk death to perpetrate a myth?"

The truth is these men are not the clandestine type. They are far more likely to be taken in by a hoax than to create one! Judas possessed the only devious mind in the group, and only God knows what has become of him.

THE DOUBTER

I still have no idea what happened to the body of Jesus, but I am quite certain none of us stole it. How to explain their newfound joy is, however, an altogether different matter.

We spend the next week in hiding, though fear is no longer our constant companion. In fact, along with the disciples newfound joy, I notice a remarkable boldness. That is not to say they do not fear for their lives, but only that the fear of dying no longer holds them hostage.

> IF THE TRUTH BE KNOWN, I AM MORE AND MORE INCLINED TO BELIEVE THAT HE IS ALIVE MYSELF.

Our days are spent reminiscing about our time with Jesus. Each day it seems we remember more, and sometimes our memories are so vivid it is almost as if Jesus himself was there with us. Of course there is constant talk about his "resurrection." They never seem to tire of it! By now I have learned that Mary Magdalene claims to have seen him first, then some of the other women. After that he supposedly appeared to Peter, then to Cleopas and his companion, and last of all, to all of them together in the upper room, just before I arrived. I am hard pressed to find a suitable explanation. At first I assumed they were hallucinating, but that hardly seems possible. There were well over a dozen people present when he allegedly appeared in the upper room on the evening of the first day of the week. It's not likely all of them were hallucinating.

If the truth be known, I am more and more inclined to believe that he is alive myself. Not only is there a remarkable consistency to their accounts, but more importantly there is the matter of the disciples' transformation. They are simply not the same. They still have their individual quirks and personality traits, but they are different somehow. More loving. More selfless.

On more than one occasion I have been tempted to proclaim my faith, to acknowledge I too believe he is alive! Something holds me back. Pride I suppose. Having declared, "Unless I see the nail marks in his hands and...put my hand into his side, I will not believe," I now find it hard to relent.

Still, more and more I hunger for the joyous assurance that comes with believing. At first I thought only those

EACH DAY SOMEONE ELSE BELIEVES AND IS TRANSFORMED.

who had actually seen him could know that joy, but now I realize how wrong I was. Each day someone else believes and is transformed. Though they have not seen him, they seem to sense his living presence and experience the joy it brings.

Now it is evening and the eleven of us are finally alone in the upper room. We have just learned that Judas hung himself,[8] a tragedy that grieves us all. Although he was not especially close to any of us, he was one of our own. I cannot bear to think of him being lost for all eternity. With deep sadness I remember the words of Jesus: "...woe to that man who betrays the Son of Man!

It would be better for him if he had not been born."[9]

I am still considering these things when suddenly the room is filled with his presence. How he got here I do not know, for the door is locked. There is no question that it is Jesus. He is readily recognizable, his appearance being much the same as it always was. Yet he is different somehow — more alive.

After bidding all of us peace he turns to me. My heart is hammering against my chest and I can hardly breath. Stretching his hands toward me he says, "Put your finger here; see my hands."[10]

Shame paints my face a bright red. Desperately I try to think of something to say, but words fail me.

Pulling open his garments he reveals a gaping wound in his side. "Reach out your hand," he commands. "Put it into my side. Stop doubting and believe."[11]

Falling to my knees, I cry, "My Lord and my God!"

With those words every doubt is resolved. I may not understand the full meaning of his death and resurrection, but of one thing I am sure — he is alive! He has conquered death, hell, and the grave!

He is only with us a short time and then he vanishes as suddenly as he appeared. My heart burns within me as I listen to the ebb and flow of conversation around me. Now that the disciples have fully accepted Jesus' resurrection they speculate about his body.

> I MAY NOT UNDERSTAND THE FULL MEANING OF HIS DEATH AND RESURRECTION, BUT OF ONE THING I AM SURE — HE IS ALIVE!

"He's not just a spirit,"[12] I say. "I touched him. He has flesh and bone just like we do."

"His body may look the same, but it's different." The speaker is Nathanael, of whom Jesus said, "Here is a true Israelite, in whom there is nothing false."[13] Being a man of few words, he usually has something substantial to say if he speaks. Now we give him our full attention.

"His body is different," he says, "but not diminished. It appears to have all the benefits of our bodies, yet without any of the limitations. It is a physical body, but not a mortal body. Apparently, He is able to experience physical pleasures like eating,[14] yet without being subject to pain or sickness. Nor is he limited by time or space."

The discussion continues around me, but I am not listening. What form his body has taken is of little concern to me. Instead, I relive that incredible moment when he stretched out his hands toward me and bid me touch him. In his presence my doubts and fears fled like darkness before the coming of day. Never again will I doubt him! Truly he is "my Lord and my God!"[15]

For further study, see Life Lessons from Chapter Eleven.

The Fisherman

...I SUDDENLY REALIZED

―――――――

IT WAS NO MERE MORTAL

―――――――

WHO SHARED MY BOAT.

CHAPTER TWELVE

The night is dark and still, the only sounds being the gentle lapping of the waves against the boat and the creak of the oars. In the bow, I am alone with my thoughts, and what a hodgepodge they are. Never have I been so confused. Try as I may I can't seem to get a handle on things. Maybe I'm just too tired to think straight.

These past weeks have been emotionally draining, leaving me numb with fatigue. One moment we are standing in dumb amazement, our mouths hanging open in disbelief as Jesus calls Lazarus back from a four-day hiatus with death.[1] The next moment we are blind with grief as Jesus dies in the darkness,[2] taking all our hopes and dreams with him.

For two nights and a day we cower in fear behind locked doors, desperately trying to find a reason to go on living. Just when we are beginning to think all is lost, Jesus puts in a surprise appearance!

We are terrified, thinking he is a ghost. Extending his hands, He shows us his wounds and says, "It's truly me.

Go ahead, touch me and see that I have flesh and bones. I am not a ghost!"[3]

Excitedly the others push forward to touch him, still not able to believe their eyes.[4] I hang back. What right do I have to be a part of this joyous celebration? Once I would have been in the thick of things or leading the way most likely, but no more. I know Jesus has forgiven me, I can see it in his eyes. The problem is, I can't forgive myself.

> WILL I EVER BE ABLE TO FORGET THE CROWING OF THE ROOSTER, I WONDER, OR THE WAY JESUS TURNED AND LOOKED AT ME?

Thinking about it now, my face burns with shame, and I am thankful for the darkness. How naive my bold promises seem in retrospect. How tragically pitiful my cowardly performance in the courtyard of Caiaphas the high priest.

Will I ever be able to forget the crowing of the rooster, I wonder, or the way Jesus turned and looked at me? Even then there was no condemnation in his eyes, only love, a faithful love — which only made my own faithlessness more insufferable. Fleeing the courtyard, I went into the night and wept bitterly.[5]

Pushing these thoughts from my mind, I consider matters at hand. It has been a wasted night for the most part, at least as far as fishing goes. Like so many other times, we have toiled all night and taken nothing. Still, it is good to return to familiar haunts.

There is something reassuring about the sound of the sea, the sweep of the sky, and the smell of the night air over open water. I had hoped to work some things out in my mind, but unfortunately the future is no less confusing.

The sky is growing light when I see a figure on the beach. I can't be sure, but he seems to be squatting beside a small fire. Looking up, he catches sight of us and calls the universal fisherman's greeting: "Have you caught anything?"

"No," someone hollers back.

"Try the other side of the boat," he says.

THE FISHERMAN

Suddenly the memory of another fruitless night of fishing comes rushing back. The same kind of nonsensical command, grudging compliance, and then a great catch of fish, so many that it threatened to capsize both boats![6]

Well do I remember trembling with a holy fear and falling at his feet, for I suddenly realized it was no mere mortal who shared my boat. Although it would be many months before I publicly declared him to be the Christ at Caesarea Philippi,[7] I think I realized it first that day. Falling to my knees I cried, "Depart from me O Lord, for I am a sinful man."[8]

CAN THAT BE ANYONE BUT JESUS STANDING THERE BESIDE THE FIRE?

But Jesus had a better idea. Instead of leaving me in my sins, he invited me to follow him. "Don't be afraid," he said. "Follow me and I will make you a fisher of men."[9]

That's how it all started, this amazing adventure. Pulling our boats up on the shore, we left everything. That is, I did, along with Andrew my brother and the sons of Zebedee. We've had some incredible times with Jesus, but nothing can match what we've been through these past few days.

Now it's happening all over again! A futile night of fishing, a ridiculous command, and another miraculous catch. Can that be anyone but Jesus standing there beside the fire? Can this be anything but his way of letting us know that nothing has changed? That our dreams are not dead? That his plans for our lives are still valid?

Once again I am overwhelmed with my own sinfulness, only this time I do not pray for him to go. Now I have a better idea. I will go to him.

Wrapping my fisher's coat around me, I throw myself into the water and swim with all my might toward shore. Staggering to my feet, I wade the last few yards, and then I am upon the beach.

Leaving the fire, he walks toward me, a huge smile lighting up his face. His eyes are laughing as he says,

"That's what I love about you, Peter. You're so outrageously impulsive."

Though I am soaking wet, he throws his arms around me and crushes me to his chest in a bear hug. Tears are coursing down my weather-beaten cheeks — not the bitter tears of remorse, which have been my daily bread since that shameful night in Caiaphas's courtyard, but the healing tears of love. If he loves me so much, how can I not love myself?

Over his shoulder I see a fire and the makings of breakfast — bread baking in the coals, fish cooking. A breeze is blowing, and it brings me the smell of wood smoke and the aroma of hot bread. Suddenly I am hungry, and I realize this is the first time I have had an appetite since we shared supper in the upper room.

Putting his arm around my shoulders, he walks me toward the water's edge, where the others are beaching the boat.

> IF HE LOVES ME SO MUCH, HOW CAN I NOT LOVE MYSELF?

Though it has been a long night, I am no longer tired. Leaping into the boat, I begin hauling the net ashore. Joyously we count the fish — one hundred and fifty-three in all — while Jesus finishes preparing breakfast.[10]

Having eaten our fill, we are lounging around the fire while the morning sun chases the last of the mist from the lake. Overhead a gull screams, and far out in the lake a fish jumps. Belatedly, I realize that I am happy, truly happy.

This is what I loved most about the three years we spent together: Those times when Jesus would say, "Let's get in the boat and find a lonely stretch of beach where we can rest." Sitting around a fire, we would talk late into the night.

Getting to his feet, Jesus motions for me to join him, cutting short my reminiscing. We walk down the beach, just the two of us. For a long time neither of us speak, then Jesus says, "Simon Peter...."

There is something about the way he calls my name that

makes my heart hurt, and I find I am holding my breath, waiting for him to continue.

"Simon Peter," he says, "do you love me more than these?"

What can I say? I love him more than I have ever loved anyone, more than I have ever loved him before. And if I do not love him with all of my heart, at least I love him with as much of it as I am capable of loving anyone. In truth, I love him more than I can say. But why should he believe me, in light of the rash promises I have made in the past?

> "SIMON PETER," HE SAYS, "DO YOU LOVE ME MORE THAN THESE?"

At last I respond, but instead of proclaiming my undying devotion I simply say, "Yes Lord. You are my dear friend, and I love you."

Once more we walk in silence, each of us emersed in his own thoughts. Then he repeats the question. "Simon, son of John, do you really love me more than these?"

Again I declare my love, being careful not to overstate my case.

Stopping, he turns toward me and looks me in the eye. It takes all the strength I have, but I meet his eyes and refuse to look away. For the third time he asks, "Simon, son of John, do you truly love me?"

Though it breaks my heart that he should question my love, I cannot blame him. Unfortunately, there is nothing I can do to restore the trust I have broken. In desperation I say, "Lord, you know all things. You know my heart better than I know it myself. Surely You know how much I love you, more than life itself."[11]

There — I have said it — "More than life itself!"

Jesus smiles and takes both of my hands in his. "Yes," he says, "I believe you do."

"When you are old Peter," he continues, "others will take you where you do not want to go."[12]

"What do you mean, Lord? I don't understand."

"Once you told me, 'Even if I have to die with you, I will never disown you.'"[13]

I remember it only too well, and I drop my eyes as the shameful memory of my denial floods my mind.

Through the pain of my regret His voice reaches me. "When you are old." he says, "you will fulfill that vow. Never again will you disown me. You will choose death first. Yes, Simon, son of John, you really do love me more than life!"[14]

Walking back toward the fire where the other disciples are napping, my heart is singing. Later I will reflect upon the death he has prophesied for me, but for now it is enough to know that I am forgiven and restored. If he trusts me, then surely I can learn to trust myself again.

> IF HE TRUSTS ME, THEN SURELY I CAN LEARN TO TRUST MYSELF AGAIN.

For further study, see Life Lessons from Chapter Twelve.

Life Lessons from Chapter One
"The Son"

The human mind cannot grasp the full ramifications of the crucifixion. It is simply beyond us. It is beyond us in the same way the eternal existence of God or the Trinity is beyond us. We accept and declare these truths by faith, but we cannot fully explain them. For instance, we know Jesus suffered the consequences of eternal damnation during the brief hours He spent on the cross, but we cannot explain how that could be.

It could not be otherwise, however. As Dr. Couch reasons, "If only the human nature of Jesus suffered, and suffered only a short time, we cannot say that His sufferings were infinite. And if His sufferings were not infinite, they could not be a satisfaction for our sins, which sins demand infinite suffering."[1]

Jesus came to the cross as "the Lamb of God, which taketh away the sin of the world."[2] He came as the Sinless One to suffer for sinful humanity, as the Righteous One to suffer for the unrighteous. But once the Roman soldiers nailed Him to the cross, a strange and terrible metamorphosis took place. The Lamb of God became a serpent;[3] the Sinless One became sin itself.[4]

That is when God discharged upon Him the full weight of His wrath, when He executed the ultimate penalty for sin — separation from Himself. In that moment Jesus heard God say, "Depart from Me." Then He cried in anguish, "My God, my God, why hast thou forsaken me?"

But He received no answer. Silence as cold as death was God's only response. However, if we dare ask God why He forsook His Son, He will answer us. "I did it for you," He says. "I did it all for you. Nothing could have been harder. It tore the very heart out of me, but there was no other way. I made Jesus a curse so you could be free from the curse of sin.[5] I made Him to be sin so you could become a saint, a new creation.[6] He had to die so you could live![7]

Life Lessons from Chapter Two
The Betrayer

Although Judas was convinced he was past saving, he was wrong. He did not need to be eternally lost. His salvation was just a prayer away. "Everyone who calls on the name of the Lord will be saved."[1] This is the promise of Scripture.

As Paul so eloquently put it, "Here is a trustworthy saying that deserves full acceptance: Christ Jesus came into the world to save sinners — of whom I am the worst. But for that very reason I was shown mercy so that in me, the worst of sinners, Christ Jesus might display his unlimited patience as an example for those who would believe on him and receive eternal life."[2]

Tragically, such love, such grace, was more than Judas could comprehend. To his flawed way of thinking, his sin was greater than God's grace. In desperation, "he went away and hanged himself."[3]

If, like Judas, you are tempted to believe you have gone too far, that your sin is past forgiving, take a moment and review the roll call of the redeemed. Jacob was a con man and thief before God changed his nature and his name. David was an adulterer and a murderer before God gave him a new heart. Peter was a foul-mouthed fisherman, Mary Magdalene a fallen woman, Zacchaeus a crooked tax collector, while Saul of Tarsus was a blasphemer and a persecutor of the church. These all received new life in Jesus Christ.

In more modern times there is John Newton, who penned the words to "Amazing Grace." He was a slave trader before Jesus redeemed him and called him into the ministry. And who could ever forget the late President Nixon's former "hatchet man," Charles Colson? Since his conversion, more than twenty years ago, he has become one of Christianity's most articulate spokesmen. These, and tens of millions like them, all stand as witnesses to the total sufficiency of God's grace.

Remember, "The Lord is compassionate and gracious, slow to anger, abounding in love....he does not treat us as our sins deserve or repay us according to our iniquities. For as high as the heavens are above the earth, so great is his love for those who fear him; as far as the east is from the west, so far has he removed our transgressions from us."[4]

Life Lessons from Chapter Three
The Governor

"Legend has it that Pilate's wife became a believer. And legend has it that Pilate's eternal home is a mountain lake where he daily surfaces, still plunging his hands into the water seeking forgiveness. Forever trying to wash away his guilt...not for the evil he did, but for the kindness he didn't do."[1]

In truth, what happened to Pilate that fateful day in Jerusalem was a foregone conclusion, the inevitable consequence of the choices of a lifetime. As the wise man writes, "...when a tree falls, whether south or north, the die is cast, for there it lies."[2]

He who repeatedly chooses expediency over character will not have the moral strength to do what is right when the ultimate test comes. The man or woman who is determined to exercise integrity in the hour of truth must practice it in the little matters that arise daily.

Life Lessons from Chapter Four
The Acquitted

Little is known about Barabbas beyond the fact that he was an insurrectionist and a murderer.[1] In truth, his anonymity suits him well, for he represents every member of our fallen race.

Was Barabbas guilty of sins against God and man? So are we. "For all have sinned and fall short of the glory of God."[2]

Was Barabbas under a sentence of death? So are we. "For the wages of sin is death."[3]

Was Barabbas undeserving of his pardon? So are we. "For it is by grace [we] have been saved, through faith — and this not from [ourselves], it is the gift of God — not by works, so that no one can boast."[4]

In the truest sense, the cross upon which Jesus died was intended not only for Barabbas, but for each of us. My sins fashioned that cross, as did yours, and it was there we should have died. But God had another idea: "While we were still sinners, Christ died for us."[5] "He himself bore our sins in his body on the tree, so that we might die to sins and live for righteousness."[6]

There is no biblical record to indicate that Barabbas ever realized the full extent of what Jesus did for him. If he did not, then Jesus was his substitute but not his Savior. Jesus died in his place, but Barabbas was not saved from his sins. What Jesus did *for* us on the cross is a sovereign work of

God, independent of anything we can do. What Jesus does *in* us through the cross is a cooperative effort between God and man. He has already died for our sins — that is, He became our substitute, He took our place — but He cannot be our Savior unless we call upon Him in faith.

Let us therefore "...confess with [our] mouth, 'Jesus is Lord,' and believe in [our] heart that God raised him from the dead, [and we] will be saved. For it is with [our] heart that [we] believe and are justified, and it is with [our] mouth that [we] confess and are saved."[7]

Life Lessons from Chapter Five
The Cyrenian

All we know for certain about Simon is that he was from Cyrene and the father of Alexander and Rufus.[1] Beyond that, we can only speculate. Still, some thoughtful speculation may be in order.

Although the Gospels of Matthew, Mark, and Luke mention Simon by name,[2] only Mark identifies him as the father of Alexander and Rufus. As anyone who has read Mark's gospel knows, he is not given to superfluous detail; therefore, we should ask ourselves why he mentions this fact, while neither Matthew nor Luke do. Undoubtedly it is because Rufus and Alexander are known to the Christians in Rome, for whom Mark's gospel was originally written.

Additional evidence supporting this conclusion is found in Paul's epistle to the believers in Rome. He writes: "Greet Rufus, chosen in the Lord, and his mother, who has been a mother to me, too."[3]

It is reasonable, I believe, to suggest that Simon's encounter with Jesus that fateful Friday was life-changing. He did not just happen to be in the "wrong place" that Passover morning, or the "right" place as it turned out. Rather, it was the grace of God that placed him there. And because Simon was entering Jerusalem at that precise moment and thus was chosen by the Roman soldier to carry our Lord's cross, his life and the lives of his family were forever altered.

Exactly when and where his conversion took place no one knows. That it did seems evident to me. And as a result of his conversion, his wife and sons apparently became Christians as well.

Life Lessons from Chapter Six
The Convicted

If you have ever questioned the validity of death-bed conversions, question no more. This converted criminal settles that issue once and for all. Though he had absolutely nothing to offer Jesus but his sins, the Lord forgave him and welcomed him into paradise.

In saving him, Jesus proved beyond question that all God

wants is us! He does not want our wealth, talent, or potential — just our hearts.

In many ways this criminal is a paradox. Though he had great faith in Jesus, he had very little faith in himself or in his value as a person. His hope rested not in what he had to offer Jesus, but in what Jesus was offering him — forgiveness and eternal life.

While those who knew Jesus best were losing their faith, this thief was finding his. While those who had heard the teaching of Jesus and witnessed His miracles were losing heart, he took heart. Though he knew nothing of the Lord's teachings or His claims to deity, he dared to trust Him with his eternal soul. "Lord," he prayed, "remember me when thou comest into thy kingdom."[1]

Yet he had very little faith in himself or his value to Jesus. He simply could not believe there was anything in him worth saving. His past was a sordid mess, his present a cruel dying, and his destiny an unmarked grave. To his way of thinking, he had absolutely nothing to recommend him to Jesus. His only hope was in the goodness of God, and there he found his salvation. "Verily," Jesus said to him, "To day shalt thou be with me in paradise."[2]

No matter what kind of mess you may have made of your life, God still loves you. Even if you are sure you have nothing to offer Him, God still wants you. Faith in yourself is not a prerequisite for salvation; you only need to have faith in Him. If you can pray, "Lord, remember me...," as this dying criminal did, Jesus will forgive your sins and save your soul.

His is the only death-bed conversion recorded in Scripture. It is there so no one need despair. It is the only one there so no one dare presume. Today is the day of salvation, so do not delay! Call upon the Lord Jesus Christ right now, "...for, Everyone who calls on the name of the Lord will be saved."[3]

Life Lessons from Chapter Seven
The Centurion

The most important question we will ever answer is the one Jesus posed to his disciples when He asked them, "Who do you say I am?"[1] Our answer will determine our eternal destiny.

Who is Jesus? Is He merely a great teacher, a prophet, or is He truly "...the Christ, the Son of the living God"?[2]

There are many who would like to accept Him as a great man or a wise teacher, but they will not believe that He is the Son of God. Such an option, however appealing, is simply not viable. If Jesus is not the Son of God as He claimed,[3] then only two options remain. Either He was a liar who falsely claimed to be divine in order to exalt Himself, or He was a mad man suffering from delusions of grandeur. Before you decide who you think He is, consider the testimony of those who knew Him best.

According to John the apostle, He is the eternal Word. John writes, "In the beginning was the Word, and the Word was with God, and the Word was God...The Word became flesh and made his dwelling among us. We have seen his glory, the glory of the One and Only, who came from the Father, full of grace and truth."[4]

Jesus' cousin, John the Baptist, said He was, "...the Lamb of God, who takes away the sin of the world!"[5]

Peter said He was, "...the Christ, the Son of the living God."[6]

Thomas called Him, "My Lord and my God!"[7]

Nathanael declared, "Rabbi, you are the Son of God; you are the King of Israel."[8]

Perhaps most convincing of all is the testimony of the centurion who commanded His crucifixion. "And when the centurion, who stood there in front of Jesus, heard his cry and saw how he died, he said, 'Surely this man was the Son of God!'"[9]

After weighing the evidence, who do you say Jesus is? Is He a liar who falsely claimed to be the Son of God? Is He a mad man suffering from delusions of grandeur? Is He a good man who is terribly deceived? Or is He divine, the Savior of the world, the Son of the living God?

Let me urge you to join with believers of all ages who affirm, in the words of the Nicene creed (fourth century): "We believe in one Lord Jesus Christ, the Son of God, only-begotten of the Father, that is, of substance of the Father, God of God, Light of Light, very God of very God, begotten not made, being of one substance with the Father; by whom all things were made which are in heaven and earth: who, for us men and for our salvation came down, and was incarnate and was made man, and suffered, and rose the third day, and ascended into the heavens, and shall come again to judge the quick and the dead."

This confession is the heart and soul of Christianity. Believe this and you will be saved, regardless of any questions you may have about creation or the infallibility of the Scriptures.

Romans 10:9 and 10 declares, "That if you confess with your mouth, 'Jesus is Lord,' and believe in your heart that God raised him from the dead, you will be saved. For it is with your heart that you believe and are justified, and it is with your mouth that you confess and are saved."

Life Lessons from Chapter Eight
The Mother

There is much for us to admire about Mary, the mother of Jesus. First there is her courage. Although we seldom consider it, Mary's obedience to the angel Gabriel's message put her at great risk. By agreeing to become the mother of Jesus she was jeopardizing her reputation, her marriage to Joseph, and her life.

In biblical times marriage consisted of three stages. First the groom's parents chose the bride and agreed with the bride's father upon the price he was to be paid. The second stage was the formal engagement or betrothal. Although the couple did not live together as husband and wife during this time, they were considered "married." The engagement could only be voided by death or divorce. The third stage was the ceremony and consummation. After the rabbi performed the service, the groom took his bride home to a room he had prepared in his father's house.

The angel Gabriel came to Mary during the second stage — while she was "pledged to be married"[1] to Joseph. At first she was "greatly troubled at his words."[2] And well she might be for once her pregnancy became known, she would be considered an unfaithful wife and the law would require Joseph to divorce her.

Should this happen she would be publicly disgraced and likely forced to sell herself into slavery or prostitution in order to support herself and her child. Nevertheless, in a supreme act of faith she surrendered to the will of God saying, "I am the Lord's servant. May it be to me as you have said."[3]

Thus begins a spiritual pilgrimage which takes her from Nazareth to Bethlehem to Egypt to Nazareth again, and ultimately to Golgotha. The hero of this story, however, is not Mary, but God the Father, who chose her to be the mother of our Lord.

According to tradition Mary was a peasant girl, probably thirteen or fourteen years old. Although she was "highly favored"[4] of God, she does not appear to have possessed any special gifts or to have been unusually spiritual, at least not until her encounter with Gabriel. In truth, she was not chosen because of her personal qualifications, but by the sovereignty of God.

The emphasis in Mary's story then, should be upon the Father, who has a long history of choosing the insignificant to accomplish the impossible. Mary's story should give each of us hope that no matter how humble our origins or how modest our present circumstances, God will use us. If God could use a humble peasant girl like Mary to give birth to the greatest miracle of all ages, then surely He can use us too.

"Brothers, think of what you were when you were called. Not many of you were wise by human standards; not many were influential; not many were of noble birth. But God chose the foolish things of the world to shame the wise; God chose the weak things of the world to shame the strong. He chose the lowly things of this world and the despised things — and things that are not — to nullify the things that are, so that no one may boast before him."[5]

Life Lessons from Chapter Nine
The Father

I think I understand the Father's agony best when I relive the Old Testament story of Abraham and Isaac. In obedience to God, Abraham takes his beloved son Isaac to Mount Moriah to sacrifice him as a burnt offering. Leaving the servants, Abraham and Isaac began the long climb toward the place of worship.

As they climb, Isaac turns to his father and says, "The fire and wood are here, but where is the lamb for the burnt offering?"[1]

How Isaac's question must tear at Abraham's heart. How desperately he must long to turn his back on that ugly mountain and return home. But he doesn't. Instead he says, "God himself will provide the lamb for the burnt offering, my son."[2]

At last they arrive at the place of sacrifice, and Abraham constructs an altar out of stones, being careful to make it both stout and level. Carefully he arranges the wood, delaying the inevitable moment as long as possible. Finally he turns toward his son.

The Scripture does not tell us what happened then. Perhaps Isaac asks again about the lamb, or maybe he has an awful premonition of what is to come and desperately searches his father's face for a reassurance that is not there. Does Abraham look his son in the eye and place his strong hands on those broad young shoulders? Do unbidden tears course down his dusty cheeks and lose themselves in his beard? Does he embrace Isaac affectionately and declare his love? Does he try to explain, to make him understand why he must do this unthinkable thing?

Or do they struggle? Does Abraham have to use force to overpower his son? Does Isaac plead for his life?

We will never know, for the Bible is silent regarding the details of those dreaded moments. It simply says, "He bound his son Isaac and laid him on the altar, on top of the wood. Then he reached out his hand and took the knife to slay his son."[3]

In my mind I see it clearly: Isaac is on the altar, bound, as still as death. Abraham is weeping, torn between his love for God and his love for his son. His hand upraised, holding the dagger, trembling, delaying its deadly descent one eternal second longer.

Suddenly the air is rent as the angel of the Lord shouts. "'Abraham! Abraham!...Do not lay a hand on the boy.'"[4] Overcome with relief, Abraham lets the deadly dagger fall to the ground. With trembling fingers he unties the knots and lifts a dazed Isaac from the altar. Cradling him in his arms like a child, he rocks back and forth saying, "My son, my son."

When at last he is able to tear his eyes from Isaac's face he sees a ram caught by its horns in a thicket. Nearly mad with joy he grabs Isaac by the hand and drags him toward the trapped animal. "Look, my son," he says. "The Lord has provided a sacrifice for the burnt offering!"

Is it too much to imagine God experiencing an agony not unlike Abraham's as He journeys with Jesus to Golgotha? Is His heart not breaking as hard Roman hands fling His Son down, position the spike, and raise the heavy hammer?

Unlike Abraham, however, there is no reprieve for God. In eternity there is only silence, for there is no other sacrifice for the sins of humanity.

What does God feel as He watches His beloved Son writhe in the agonies of a slow death? Does He not long to tear the darkness away, to gently lift the trembling body of Jesus from the cross, to heal his wounds, to restore him to his place of preeminence?

Undoubtedly He does, but He does not intervene. For as great as His love is for His Son, greater still is His love for our lost race. "But God demonstrates his own love for us in this: While we were still sinners, Christ died for us."[5]

When the two malefactors who were crucified with Jesus witnessed His sacrificial love, they responded in distinctly different ways. "One of the criminals who hung there hurled insults at him: 'Aren't you the Christ? Save yourself and us!'

"But the other criminal rebuked him. 'Don't you fear God,' he said, 'since you are under the same sentence? We are punished justly for we are getting what our deeds deserve. But this man has done nothing wrong.'

"Then he said, 'Jesus, remember me when you come into your kingdom.'"[6]

One of them rejected His love and was lost, while the other received His love and was saved. What will you do? If, like the penitent malefactor, you are moved to respond to His love, let me urge you to call upon His name and be saved. For "Salvation is found in no one else, for there is no other name under heaven given to men by which we must be saved."[7]

Life Lessons from Chapter Ten
The Harlot

One cannot read the New Testament without realizing that Jesus had a special ministry to women. He understood their unique needs in a way no man ever had.

He felt their longings, sensed their pain, and shared their sorrows. With compassion He met them at the point of their need and ministered life unto them.

Such sensitivity would be remarkable in any circumstance, but given the conditions under which women lived in Jesus day, it becomes even more impressive. Women had no rights. Before marriage they were considered the property of their father, and following marriage they became the property of their husband. Their testimony was not accepted in a court of law, nor could they own property.

Jesus ministered not only to individual women, but to women as a whole. He treated them as full-fledged human beings with all the rights of citizens in the kingdom of God. As far as He was concerned, they were equal in value to men, just different in function.

In ministering to Mary Magdalene, Jesus violated all the prohibitions of the religious leaders of His day. Not only was she a woman — which automatically made her a second-class citizen — but she was also demon possessed.[1] Given these facts, it is not hard to see why the religious leaders considered her a lost cause. To their way of thinking, her kind was not worth saving.

But Jesus saw things differently. Instead of giving up on her, He redeemed her and made her the first missionary of the resurrection. He appeared to her first after His resurrection[2] and commanded her, "Go...to my brothers and tell them, 'I am returning to my Father and your Father, to my God and your God.'"[3]

There is, I believe, a message in her story for everyone. It is our Lord's way of saying that none of us are so lost that we cannot be found, nor so sinful that we cannot be forgiven. Even if everyone else has given up on us, He hasn't. Even if we give up on ourselves, He will never give up on us!

"For the Son of Man came to seek and to save what was lost."[4]

Life Lessons from Chapter Eleven
The Doubter

It is a mistake to think of Thomas primarily as a pessimist and a doubter. For three years he was a faithful follower of Jesus, and as the end drew near he was the one who courageously urged the others to return with Jesus to Judea regardless of the risks. "Let us also go," he said, "that we may die with him."[1]

Nor was he the only disciple to question the validity of the resurrection. Mark tells us that "When they (the other disciples) heard that Jesus was alive and that she (Mary Magdalene) had seen him, they did not believe it."[2] Apparently they too found the truth "too good to be true."[3] Each resurrection appearance was initially greeted with skepticism. For example, Mary Magdalene mistook Him for the gardener,[4] the eleven thought He was a ghost,[5] and the two on the road to Emmaus were sure He was just another pilgrim until He opened their eyes.[6]

Rather than diminishing the resurrection, their doubts actually enhance it. These were not starry-eyed dreamers expecting a resurrection, but disillusioned disciples who had lost all hope. The fact that they became passionate apologists for the resurrection is nearly as astounding as the empty tomb itself.

Let me interject here that doubt is not a bad thing as much as it is a real thing. And let us always be careful to distinguish between doubt and unbelief. Doubt is an involuntary emotion while unbelief is an act of the will.

Doubt inevitably yields to the power of His presence, as in the case of Thomas who cried, "My Lord and my God!"[7] Unbelief, on the other hand, hardens into rebellion. The unbeliever chooses not to believe regardless of the evidence.

Following the gospel accounts, Thomas vanishes from the pages of Scripture. Tradition, however, teaches that he became a missionary of the resurrection, spreading the gospel in Parthia and Persia, where he died. Later tradition places him in India, where he was martyred. Whichever account we accept, it is obvious that this doubting disciple was transformed by the resurrection of Jesus.

Many of the things God promises to those who trust Him seem almost too good to be true, like forgiveness,[8] a new life,[9] fellowship with Him,[10] and eternal life.[11] Still, if we will invite Jesus to inhabit all the dark, doubt-filled corners in our lives, He will fill us with the wonder of His presence. Like Thomas, we will exclaim, "My Lord and my God."[12]

Life Lessons from Chapter Twelve
The Fisherman

No one in all of the Bible is more beloved than Simon Peter, and with good reason. He is incredibly real. We can identify with him, especially his blunders. Like him we have all stuck our foot in our mouth, made promises we couldn't keep, and ended up failing shamefully.

And like Peter, we have had our moments in the sun, moments when the truth of revelation has broken through, infusing our mundane lives with the light of God's eternal glory. Still, it is Peter's failures that most endear him to our hearts, that give us our best hope.

If all we knew of Peter were his triumphs — those moments when his faith shown with other-worldly brilliance — he would be an intimidating figure indeed. By the same token, if all we knew of him were his failures — those times when he was so obviously human — he would be forgettable at best. But when we see the whole Peter, with both his strengths and weaknesses, he is an inspiration to us.

As I consider Peter's life and ministry, two things seem to stand out above all the rest. First, God's ability to use ordinary people to accomplish extraordinary things. Peter was no towering intellect, nor was he a man of extraordinary insight or courage. He was a working man, a fisherman. This is the very thing that makes him so remarkable. He is so much like us. And if God could use an ordinary man like Peter, then surely He can use ordinary people like you and me.

The second thing that stands out has more to do with God than with Peter. No matter how many times Peter failed, God refused to give up on him. God had a plan for his life and He refused to allow Peter's repeated failures to compromise His divine purposes.

In the end God redeemed Peter's mistakes; that is, He touched them with His redeeming grace and caused them to contribute to Peter's ultimate Christlikeness. And if God did not reject Peter because of his mistakes, He will not reject us either. In truth, "God's gifts and his call are irrevocable."[1]

Ultimately Peter became one of the foremost apostles in the early church. He was the first apostle to witness the resurrection.[2] He preached the first Christian message on the day of Pentecost.[3] He was the first apostle to preach salvation to the Gentiles when he preached at the house of Cornelius, the Roman centurion.[4]

Papias, writing about A.D. 125, stated that Peter's preaching inspired the writing of the first gospel, drafted by Mark, who was Peter's interpreter in Rome. He is also the author of the two epistles which bear his name. Quite a list of accomplishments for such an ordinary man, especially one who denied Jesus three times and the third time with a curse.[5]

Tradition tells us that Peter died a martyr's death in Rome. In the end he asked only one thing: that he might be crucified with his head down, as he was not worthy to be crucified in the same manner as his Lord.

Endnotes

Chapter One: *The Son*

[1] 2 Corinthians 5:21.

[2] Isaiah 53:3-10.

[3] Mark 14:34.

[4] Mark 14:36.

[5] Mark 14:37.

[6] Mark 14:40.

[7] Mark 14:38.

[8] Luke 22:44.

[9] Matthew 26:42.

[10] Hebrews 5:7.

[11] Hebrews 4:15.

[12] Mark 14:42.

[13] Luke 22:48.

[14] John 18:10.

[15] Luke 22:51.

[16] Luke 22:52-53.

[17] John 18:12.

[18] Matthew 27:45.

[19] Matthew 27:46.

[20] Luke 23:46.

Chapter Two: *The Betrayer*

[1] Matthew 16:16.
[2] Matthew 19:28.
[3] John 18:13.
[4] John 21:25.
[5] Mark 14:56.
[6] John 18:15-16.
[7] Matthew 26:63.
[8] Matthew 8:23-27.
[9] Luke 7:11-16.
[10] John 11:38-44.
[11] Matthew 26:64.
[12] Matthew 26:66.
[13] Ibid.
[14] Matthew 26:67-68.
[15] Matthew 27:4.
[16] Ibid.
[17] Matthew 27:5.
[18] Matthew 26:24.
[19] Ibid.
[20] Matthew 27:5.

Chapter Three: *The Governor*

[1]See Josephus, "Antiquities of the Jews, xviii, 3, 1," quoted in *The Light of the Cross* by S. Barton Babbage (Grand Rapids: Zondervan Publishing House, 1966), pp. 12,13.

[2]John 18:28-38.

[3]Matthew 27:19.

[4]Luke 23:13-17.

[5]John 18:40.

[6]See Jim Bishop, *The Day Christ Died* (New York: Harper & Brothers, 1957), p. 294.

[7]John 19:1-15.

[8]Matthew 27:24.

[9]Matthew 27:25.

[10]Ibid.

Chapter Four: *The Acquitted*

[1]Luke 23:28-30.

Chapter Five: *The Cyrenian*

[1]See Jim Bishop, *The Day Christ Died* (New York: Harper & Brothers, 1957), p. 277.

[2]Isaiah 53:2-3.

Chapter Six: *The Convicted*

[1] Isaiah 53:12.
[2] Isaiah 53:6.
[3] Luke 23:39.
[4] Luke 23:40-41.
[5] Luke 23:42.
[6] Luke 23:43.
[7] 2 Corinthians 5:17.
[8] Luke 15:10.

Chapter Seven: *The Centurion*

[1] John 19:19.
[2] John 19:20.
[3] John 1:46.
[4] Luke 23:34.
[5] Isaiah 53:7.
[6] See Bishop, *The Day Christ Died*, pp. 292-298.
[7] Matthew 27:46.
[8] Ibid.
[9] John 19:30.
[10] Luke 23:46.
[11] Mark 15:39.

Chapter Eight: *The Mother*

[1] See Roger L. Fredrikson, *The Communicator's Commentary, Volume 4: John* (Waco: Word Books, Publisher, 1985), p. 275.

[2] Leviticus 12:1-8.

[3] Luke 2:34.

[4] Luke 2:35.

[5] Matthew 2:16.

[6] Matthew 2:13.

[7] John 1:29.

[8] Luke 3:22.

[9] Luke 4:18.

[10] Luke 4:21.

[11] Mark 6:3.

[12] Luke 4:29-30.

[13] Matthew 4:13.

[14] John 19:14.

[15] John 19:15.

[16] Luke 23:35.

[17] Mark 15:29-30,32.

[18] Luke 23:34.

[19] John 19:26.

[20] John 19:27.

Chapter Nine: *The Father*

[1] Revelation 13:8.
[2] Mark 14:36.
[3] Matthew 26:39.
[4] Luke 22:43.
[5] Luke 22:44.
[6] Mark 14:36.
[7] Matthew 26:42.
[8] Mark 15:33.
[9] Leviticus 16:21.
[10] 2 Corinthians 5:21.
[11] Ibid.
[12] Mark 15:34.
[13] Isaiah 53.
[14] Luke 23:46.
[15] Mark 15:38.
[16] Isaiah 1:18.

Chapter Ten: *The Harlot*

[1] See the account of the resurrection in this chapter is based entirely on John 20:1-18.

[2] Matthew 16:16.

[3] Mark 16:9.

[4] John 20:1-13.

[5] John 20:15.

[6] John 20:16.

[7] John 20:17.

[8] Matthew 28:20.

Chapter Eleven: *The Doubter*

[1] Thomas — also called Didymus, the Greek word for "twin." (See John 20:24.) *Nelson's Illustrated Bible Dictionary* (Nashville: Thomas Nelson, Inc., 1986).

[2] John 11:53-57.

[3] John 12:23-24.

[4] John 11:16.

[5] John 20:25.

[6] Luke 24:13-35.

[7] Matthew 28:11-15.

[8] Matthew 27:3-10.

[9] Mark 14:21.

[10] John 20:27.

[11] Ibid.

[12] Luke 24:39.

[13] John 1:47.

[14] Luke 24:43.

[15] John 20:28.

Chapter Twelve: *The Fisherman*

[1]John 11:38-45.
[2]Luke 23:44-46.
[3]Luke 24:36-39.
[4]Luke 24:40.
[5]Luke 22:61-62.
[6]Luke 5:1-6.
[7]Matthew 16:13-20.
[8]Luke 5:8.
[9]Luke 5:10 and Mark 1:17.
[10]John 21:7-12.
[11]John 21:15-17.
[12]John 21:18.
[13]Mark 14:31.
[14]John 21:18-19.

Life Lessons from Chapter One: *The Son*

[1] See Robert G. Lee, D.D., LL.D., *The Saviour's Seven Statements From The Cross* (Grand Rapids: Zondervan Publishing House, 1968), p. 91.

[2] John 1:29 (KJV).

[3] John 3:14.

[4] 2 Corinthians 5:21.

[5] Galatians 3:13.

[6] 2 Corinthians 5:17,21.

[7] Hebrews 9:15.

Life Lessons from Chapter Two: *The Betrayer*

[1] Romans 10:13.

[2] 1 Timothy 1:15-16.

[3] Matthew 27:5.

[4] Psalm 103:8,10-12.

Life Lessons from Chapter Three: *The Governor*

[1] See Max Lucado, *The Final Week of Jesus* (Portland: Multnomah Books, 1994), p. 106.

[2] Ecclesiastes 11:3 (TLB).

Life Lessons from Chapter Four: *The Acquitted*

[1] Luke 23:25.
[2] Romans 3:23.
[3] Romans 6:23.
[4] Ephesians 2:8-9.
[5] Romans 5:8.
[6] 1 Peter 2:24.
[7] Romans 10:9-10.

Life Lessons from Chapter Five: *The Cyrenian*

[1] Mark 15:21.
[2] Matthew 27:32, Mark 15:21, and Luke 23:26.
[3] Romans 16:13.

Life Lessons from Chapter Six: *The Convicted*

[1] Luke 23:42 (KJV).
[2] Luke 23:43 (KJV).
[3] Romans 10:13.

Life Lessons from Chapter Seven: *The Centurion*

[1] Matthew 16:15.
[2] Matthew 16:16.
[3] Matthew 26:63-64.
[4] John 1:1,14.
[5] John 1:29.
[6] Matthew 16:16.
[7] John 20:28.
[8] John 1:49.
[9] Mark 15:39.

Life Lessons from Chapter Eight: *The Mother*

[1] Luke 1:27.
[2] Luke 1:29.
[3] Luke 1:38.
[4] Luke 1:28.
[5] 1 Corinthians 1:26-29.

Life Lessons from Chapter Nine: *The Father*

[1] Genesis 22:7.
[2] Genesis 22:8.
[3] Genesis 22:9-10.
[4] Genesis 22:11-12.
[5] Romans 5:8.
[6] Luke 23:39-42.
[7] Acts 4:12.

Life Lessons from Chapter Ten: *The Harlot*

[1] Luke 8:2.

[2] Mark 16:9.

[3] John 20:17.

[4] Luke 19:10.

Life Lessons from Chapter Eleven: *The Doubter*

[1] John 11:16.

[2] Mark 16:11.

[3] Luke 24:37-45.

[4] John 20:15.

[5] Luke 24:37.

[6] Luke 24:13-32.

[7] John 20:28.

[8] 1 John 1:9.

[9] 2 Corinthians 5:17.

[10] 1 John 1:7.

[11] 1 John 5:11-13.

[12] John 20:28.

Life Lessons from Chapter Twelve: *The Fisherman*

[1] Romans 11:29.

[2] 1 Corinthians 15:5-8.

[3] Acts 2:14-41.

[4] Acts 10:23-48.

[5] Mark 14:66-72.

Other Books by Richard Exley:

Straight from the Heart for Christmas
Straight from the Heart for Mom
Straight from the Heart for Dad
Straight from the Heart for Graduates
Straight from the Heart for Couples
How to be a Man of Character in a World of Compromise
Marriage in the Making
The Making of A Man
Life's Bottom Line
Perils of Power
The Rhythm of Life
When You Lose Someone You Love
The Other God — Seeing God as He Really Is
The Painted Parable
Whispers of the Heart for the One I Love

For a complete list of our titles, visit our website:
www.whitestonebooks.com

WHITE STONE BOOKS
LAKELAND, FLORIDA